OUTLINES OF ELECTROCHEMISTRY

MAXWELL PRESS

OUTLINES OF ELECTROCHEMISTRY

HARRY C. JONES

Associate Professor of Physical Chemistry in the
Johns Hopkins University

MAXWELL PRESS

Chennai   Trichy   NewDelhi

MAXWELL PRESS

This edition has been published in india by arrangement with Carson Books, UK

ISBN 978-93-90063-92-5   Maxwell Press

MJP 935   © Publishers, 2023

Publisher's Note

The legacy of a country is in its varied cultural heritage, historical literature, developments in the field of economy and science. The top nations in the world are competing in the field of science, economy and literature. This vast legacy has to be conserved and documented so that it can be bestowed to the future generation. The knowledge of this legacy is slowly getting perished in the present generation due to lack of documentation.

Keeping this in mind, the concern with retrospective acquiring of rare books has been accented recently by the burgeoning reprint industry. Maxwell Press is gratified to retrieve the rare collections with a view to bring back those books that were landmarks in their time.

In this effort, a series of rare books would be republished under the banner, "Maxwell Press". The books in the reprint series have been carefully selected for their contemporary usefulness as well as their historical importance within the intellectual. We reconstruct the book with slight enhancements made for better presentation, without affecting the contents of the original edition.

Most of the works selected for republishing covers a huge range of subjects, from history to anthropology. We believe this reprint edition will be a service to the numerous researchers and practitioners active in this fascinating field. We allow readers to experience the wonder of peering into a scholarly work of the highest order and seminal significance.

MAXWELL PRESS

TABLE OF CONTENTS.

INTRODUCTION.

The term electrochemistry is used to-day so frequently, not only in pure science, but in the technical world, that we should inquire just what it means. This is the more desirable since we frequently find it employed rather loosely to embrace a multitude of phenomena, some of which have very little to do with the subject. We can see the significance of this term more clearly by studying the early development of the subject, than by any definition, which would probably include terms less familiar than the word which we are trying to define. In the latter part of the eighteenth century Volta discovered the pile which bears his name. This consists of two metals and an acid, and from such a combination electricity can be obtained. When this pile acts—i. e., produces electricity—the metal is used up and the acid also is used up. The substances present in the pile undergo serious chemical change, and the result is the production of electricity. These facts show that there is some close connection between the chemical action going on in the cell and the production of the electricity.

If, now, the electricity thus produced is conducted through solutions of certain substances, serious changes take place. If it is passed through a solution of copper sulphate, metallic copper is deposited upon one of the poles, and if these are of platinum, free sulphuric acid is formed around the other pole. This fact alone would indicate that the current has the power to decompose chemical substances, or, as we say, to overcome the chemical attraction which holds them together. It was easily recognized that there is some close connection between electricity and chemical attraction, but no clear conception of this relation could be formed until the discovery of the laws of the correlation and conservation of energy by Mayer and Joule, and the subsequent development of this whole subject by Helmholtz. Our present conceptions of energy relations, which are the direct outgrowth of this work, furnish us with a clear picture of what takes place in the experiments described above.

In the voltaic pile we have chemical energy converted into electrical. The metal passes from a condition of greater chemical energy to one of less, and the difference between the chemical energy in the system before and after the cell has acted, is converted, for the most part, into electrical energy. The chemical energy which has disappeared during the action of the cell is converted chiefly into electrical energy. This is clearly an example of the transformation of chemical energy into electrical.

When, on the other hand, a current is passed through a solution of a salt like copper sulphate, the metal is deposited in a form containing a larger amount of chemical energy than when present in the salt. We also have electrical energy used up in effecting the electrolysis of the salt.

In this case we have, then, a transformation of electrical energy into chemical energy.

The above experiments illustrate the mutual transformability of chemical and electrical energies, and this furnishes the subject matter of electrochemistry.

THE DEVELOPMENT OF ELECTRO-CHEMISTRY.

Phenomena which belong to electrochemistry were studied during the entire nineteenth century. The work of Humphrey Davy on the electrolysis of the alkalies, which he effected by means of his large voltaic pile at the very beginning of the century, attracted attention to this field of investigation, and much of the best work of Faraday was done along strictly electrochemical lines. He was particularly interested in the decompositions effected by the current, and it is difficult to overestimate the importance of his investigations in this field on the subsequent development of electrochemistry.

In connection with the development of the theoretical side of electrochemistry Berzelius will always be prominent. His electrochemical theory, which is recognized to-day to contain the germ of a great truth, exercised a powerful influence on men of science during the first half of the nineteenth century, and attracted attention to electrochemistry as throwing light on the all-important problem of chemical combination.

Many other illustrious names might be mentioned in connection with the earlier development of electrochemistry. That of Hittorf must not be omitted. It was he, as we shall learn, who first pointed out a method of measuring the relative velocities with which the ions travel; and F.

Kohlrausch furnished us with the first reliable method of measuring the conductivity of solutions, but space will not permit us to go farther in this connection.

THE NEW ELECTROCHEMISTRY.

The electrochemistry of to-day, as we shall learn, differs in many respects from that of the earlier period. Like the older work it deals with the reciprocal transformations of chemical and electrical energy, but deals with them by entirely new methods. These are the outcome of certain generalizations which were reached in 1886 and 1887, and which have thrown entirely new light over the whole field of chemistry. These generalizations are, *that the laws of gas-pressure apply to the osmotic pressure of solutions; and that electrolytes in the presence of water are largely dissociated into ions.*

It would be impossible to follow the more recent developments in electrochemistry, without a comprehensive grasp of the meaning and significance of these generalizations. They are, therefore, considered at some length in the following chapters. The recent applications of these generalizations to electrochemical problems, constitute the subject matter of the later chapters of this book.

A word in reference to the relations of electrochemistry to the broader subject of which it is a part—physical chemistry. Since the generalizations referred to above were discovered, a new branch of science occupying a position between physics and chemistry, has come into prominence. This is known as physical chemistry.

Physical chemistry to-day does not mean simply the study of the physical properties of chemical compounds, as it did formerly, but has to do chiefly with the energy transformations which take place in chemical reactions. The heat changes which always occur when substances react chemically are studied under thermochemistry—an important chapter of physical chemistry.

Physical chemistry is especially concerned with the properties of substances in solution—the condition under which most chemical reactions take place. It includes also the study of the velocity of chemical reactions, and the conditions under which chemical reactions come to rest, or are in equilibrium. Finally, it includes the study of the transformations of chemical and electrical energy—in a word, electrochemistry.

We thus see the relation of electrochemistry to the several chapters of which physical chemistry is composed.

OUTLINES OF ELECTROCHEMISTRY.

CHAPTER I—OSMOTIC PRESSURE.

INTRODUCTION.

IT IS WELL KNOWN that in the last few years a new branch of science has come into existence. Since the phenomena with which it deals lie midway between physics and chemistry, it is called physical chemistry, and to distinguish it from the older physical chemistry, from which it differs fundamentally and in kind, it has been termed the new physical chemistry.

This subject embraces a number of chapters, such as the study of atoms and molecules, of solids, liquids, and gases, of thermochemistry, electrochemistry, chemical dynamics and statics, etc. That portion of physical chemistry which concerns us here has to do with the transformations of chemical energy into electrical, and of electric energy into chemical, and this constitutes the subject matter of electrochemistry.

It is not the intention of these papers to treat the subject of electrochemistry in a systematic or exhaustive manner, as would be done in an advanced text-book on this subject, but to take up certain sections which seem particularly interesting and important.

It would be impossible to plunge intelligibly into the subject matter of electrochemistry, without first studying some phenomena which lie at the foundation of all electrochemistry, and upon which it rests. We shall take up first the phenomena connected with osmotic pressure, and point out certain relations between the osmotic pressure exerted by solutions and other physical phenomena which are well known.

WHAT IS MEANT BY OSMOTIC PRESSURE.

It was known from the earliest time that when certain solid substances are brought in contact with certain liquids, the former dissolve, and when quantitative methods began to be discovered, it was soon found that such substances distributed themselves uniformly throughout the solvent. This phenomenon was called diffusion, but the cause of diffusion was entirely unknown. Why does the dissolved substance pass into every portion of the solvent until the whole solution becomes homogeneous, each equal volume containing the same amount of the dissolved substance? The question could not be answered. This was all the more perplexing, when it was considered that substances much heavier than the solvent would rise from the bottom of the containing-vessel into the solvent, right against the pull of gravity. Another fact which had been known for a long time is that an animal bladder, when filled with a mixture of alcohol and water and plunged into pure water, will swell up and burst. It was obvious that there is some pressure manifesting itself in this case, and such has been termed *osmotic pressure*.

A pressure similar to the above was found to exist at the surface of contact of every solution with the pure solvent, and also at the surface of contact of every solution of a substance with every other solution of different concentration. These observations are, of course, purely qualitative, but, like the study of every phenomenon in science, we have first the qualitative observations and then the quantitative measurements. The earlier observers had no conception as to the magnitude of the osmotic pressure which a solution will exert, and no idea how it could be measured.

THE MEASUREMENT OF OSMOTIC PRESSURE.

If we were dependent upon animal membranes or upon any other natural membrane to measure the magnitude of osmotic pressure, our knowledge of this subject would be most unsatisfactory. But artificial membranes, which can stand many times the pressure of any natural membrane, have been prepared and used successfully to measure the magnitude of the osmotic pressure exerted by not too concentrate solutions.

In order that any membrane may be used to measure osmotic pressure it must allow the pure solvent to pass through, but prevent the dissolved substance from passing. Thus, in the case of a solution of cane sugar in water, the membrane must allow the water to pass readily through, but must be impervious to the cane sugar molecules. The reason for this is obvious. If the membrane which separated the solutions of different concentrations allowed the dissolved substance to pass through, the solutions on the two sides would by diffusion become of the same concentration, and no osmotic pressure would exist between them. Such membranes, whioh are permeable to the solvent but are impermeable to the dissolved substance, are known as *semi-permeable membranes.*

It has been found that certain precipitates have this property of allowing water to pass through them, but of preventing certain substances, like cane sugar. Among these should be mentioned copper ferro-cyanide, the precipitate formed when a solution of potassium ferrocyanide is brought in contact with a solution of a soluble copper salt, say copper sulphate. The reaction is expressed by the following equation

$$K_4Fe(CN)_6 + 2CuSO_4 = Cu_2Fe(CN)_6 + 2K_2SO_4.$$

A number of other substances, such as calcium phosphate, Berlin blue, etc., have been found to have the same property to some extent.

In order that such a precipitate should be used to measure osmotic pressure it must be given a resistant support, and the following device has been adopted. The precipitate was deposited right in the walls of a fine-grained, porcelain cup, by filling the cup with a solution of potassium ferrocyanide and immersing it in a solution of copper sulphate. Where the two solutions came together in the walls of the cup the precipitate was formed, and had the property of semi-permcability, whioh is essential to the measurement of osmotic pressure.

In preparing these membranes great care and patience are necessary to work out the details, but this is not the place to discuss these details.*

Having prepared the cell containing the semi-permeable membrane, it was filled with the solution whose osmotic pressure was to be measured, and tightly closed by means of a cork, through which a manometer passed. The cell containing the solution was then immersed in a vessel containing pure water. The water passed through the semi-permeable membrane into the cup, and produced a pressure which could be read on the manometer.

* See Pfeffer's monograph on Osmotische Untersuchungen. L-ipzig, 1877.

Water would continue to flow in until the hydrostatic pressure on the inside was just equal to the osmotic pressure which the solution was capable of exerting against the pure solvent. By reading the maximum pressure produced, by means of the manometer, we have the osmotic pressure of the solution which is equal to it.

RESULTS OF THE MEASUREMENT OF OSMOTIC PRESSURE.

The first fact which was noticed as the result of the quantitative study of osmotic

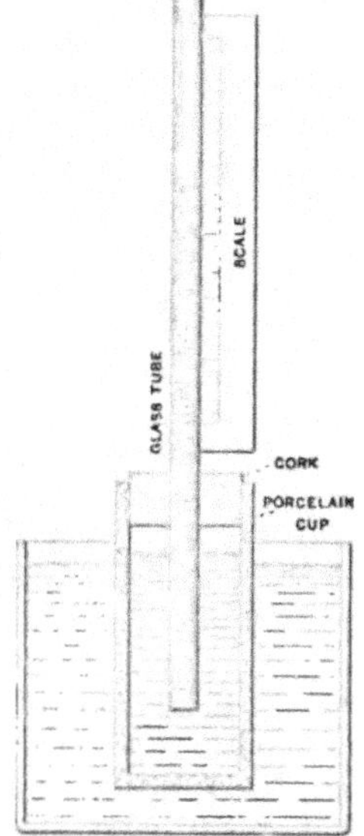

FIG. 1.—DETERMINATION OF OSMOTIC PRESSURE.

pressure, was the enormous magnitude of the pressure which even dilute solutions can exert. From the earlier observations on osmotic pressure, by means of which an animal bladder was burst when it was filled with a fairly concentrated solution of alcohol, the conclusion was drawn that in osmotic pressure we have to deal with

an appreciable force; but no one imagined for a moment that the magnitude of the force was as great as it is. Pfeffer, who is now Professor of Botany in the University of Leipzig, found that a tenth-normal* solution of cane sugar in water has an osmotic pressure of about two atmospheres. If an open water manometer was used, the column of water would rise to a height of about 66 feet.

Pfeffer studied the osmotic pressures of solutions of a number of substances at different concentrations, and a few of his results are given below to illustrate certain relations which will be pointed out a little later:

CANE SUGAR.

Concentration in Per Cent by Weight.	Osmotic Pressure.
1	535 mm. Hg
2	1,016
4	2,082
6	3,075

Pfeffer also studied the effect of temperature on the osmotic pressure of a solution of cane sugar. He used a one per cent solution, and measured its osmotic pressure at different temperatures. He obtained the following results:

Temperature.	Osmotic Pressure.
14°.2 C	510 mm. Hg.
32°.0 C	544
6°.8 C	505
13°.7 C	525
22°.0 C	548
15°.5 C	520
36°.0 C	567

Pfeffer was studying osmotic pressure from the standpoint of a botanist, and the remainder of his work has to do chiefly with the botanical significance of his measurements. He did not point out any relations between the osmotic pressure of

---

* A normal solution of cane sugar is one which contains a gram-molecular weight — 342.1 grams, in a litre.

solutions and the gas-pressure of gases. This remained for another.

RELATIONS BETWEEN OSMOTIC PRESSURE AND GAS-PRESSURE.

That there was any relation between the osmotic pressure of a solution and the gas-pressure of a gas, was not suspected until the epoch-making paper* of the great Dutch physical chemist, Van't Hoff, appeared in 1887. This paper bears the title "The Role of Osmotic Pressure in the Analogy between Solutions and Gases," and the title is self explanatory

Van't Hoff's† attention was called to the experimental work of Pfeffer by his colleague in the University of Amsterdam— the botanist De Vries,—and he took up a study of Pfeffer's results in connection with certain other problems in which he was interested at that time,‡ He was at once impressed by the relation between the osmotic pressures of concentrations. The creases with the concentration of the solution, and the important point is that the osmotic pressure increases proportional to the concentration. This can be seen at once, if we divide the osmotic pressures of the different solutions by the percentage concentrations of the solutions, as Van't Hoff did. The following results will illustrate the point. If we represent the concentrations by C, and the osmotic pressures by P; P divided by C is a constant:

C	$\dfrac{P}{C}$
1%	535
2%	508
4%	521
6%	513

* *Ztschr. phys Chem* 1, 481 English by H C Jones, *Science Memoir Series*, vol. iv, p 13 (Amer. Book Co.)
† Van't Hoff was at that time Professor of Chemistry in Amsterdam. He is now Professor of Physical Chemistry in the University of Berlin.
‡ For further detail see Theory of Electrolytic Dissociation by H. C. Jones (Macmillan's)

The value of $\dfrac{P}{C}$ is as nearly constant as could be expected, when we consider the difficulties and large experimental errors which are necessarily involved in all measurements of osmotic pressure.

Of what scientific value was the discovery of this relation? Would it not, after all, be just what we should expect? If one molecule exerts a given osmotic pressure, would not two molecules exert twice this pressure, three molecules three times the pressure, and n molecules n times the pressure? This is just what is expressed by the above relation; but to a mind of the type of that of Van't Hoff it meant a great deal more. He saw in this relation an analogy to the *Law of Boyle for Gases.* This law says that the pressure exerted by a gas is proportional to the concentration of the gas.

It seemed, then, from these few results that the *Law of Boyle for Gas-pressure Applies to the Osmotic Pressure of Solution,* and that the two kinds of pressure were analogous, at least in this one respect, that they were proportional, on the one hand to the concentration of the solution, on the other to the concentration of the gas.

Having found that the law of Boyle for gas-pressure applies to the osmotic pressure of solutions, Van't Hoff naturally began to look around for other analogies between the two kinds of pressure. We have seen that the osmotic pressure of a solution increases with increase in temperature, and it is well known that the gas-pressure of a gas increases with increase in temperature. Does any relation exist between the amount by which the osmotic pressure is increased, and the amount by which gas-pressure is increased? This would be tested by studying the pressure of a gas at a given temperature, and then at a somewhat higher temperature, and observing the increase in pressure for a given increase in temperature. This, as is well known, has been very carefully done, and the results have led to the generalization known as the law of Gay Lussac, which says that the pressure of a gas increases a constant amount for every increase in temperature of one degree; and the increase in pressure amounts to one-two hundred and seventy-third of the original pressure of the gas at zero Centigrade. To test this law for osmotic pressure we should naturally proceed as follows: The osmotic pressure of a solution would be measured at a given temperature, and then measured again at a somewhat higher temperature, and the difference between the two pressures noted. The difference between the two temperatures would also be noted, and from these data we could calculate at once the increase in osmotic pressure for a rise in temperature of one degree.

This is exactly what has been done by Pfeffer, as will be seen by examining the second set of his results, given in an earlier part of this paper. If we divide the difference between the osmotic pressures at any two temperatures by the difference in temperatures, we shall find that the value is not exactly the same for different experiments, and is not one-two hundred and seventy-third of the original osmotic pressure. This might at first be interpreted to mean that the law of Gay Lussac does not apply to the osmotic pressure of solutions, but we must again consider the enormous difficulties involved in making good semi-permeable membranes, and in carrying out osmotic pressure de-

terminations with even a fair degree of accuracy. Taking all of these matters into account, and, further, that the temperature coefficient of osmotic pressure found from the results of Pfeffer, always approached the value one-two hundred and seventy-third, Van't Hoff concluded that it was probable that the law of Gay Lussac for the temperature coefficient of gas-pressure applied to the osmotic pressure of solutions.

Van't Hoff, however, made use of another principle in testing the law of Gay Lussac, as applied to the osmotic pressure of solutions. If a gas were placed in a closed glass tube and the two ends of the tube kept at different temperatures, the gas would distribute itself throughout the tube, so that the pressure would be the same at every point. In the warmer portion of the tube a gas molecule would exert a greater pressure than in the cooler portion, and, consequently, the gas would tend to become more dilute in the warmer portion and more concentrated in the cooler portion of the tube. The difference in concentration could be calculated theoretically from the law of Gay Lussac, knowing the difference between the temperatures of the two ends of the tube.

If a tube is filled with a homogeneous solution and one end kept at a higher temperature than the other, the solution will become more dilute in the region where the temperature is higher. This is known as *the Principle of Soret*. If the law of Gay Lussac applies to the temperature coefficient of the osmotic pressure of solutions, we could calculate the difference in concentration between the warmer and colder portions of the tube, knowing the difference in the temperatures; just as we can calculate the difference in the concentrations of a gas, as described above.

The experiments were carried out by filling glass tubes with a homogeneous solution, and keeping the tops of the tubes at a higher constant temperature than the bottoms. After the tubes had stood for what was supposed to be a sufficient length of time, a measured volume of the solution was removed from the top and analyzed, and a measured volume removed from the bottom and also analyzed. Knowing the concentration of the original homogeneous solution, and the difference between the concentrations at the top and bottom of the tube, we have all the data necessary for testing the Principle of Soret, as applied to solutions.

The results at first showed smaller differences in concentration for a given difference in temperature, than would be expected if the law of Gay Lussac applied to the temperature coefficient of the osmotic pressure of solutions. It then occurred to Soret and others that perhaps the solution had not been allowed to stand long enough at the different, constant, temperatures, in order that equilibrium should be reached. It is well known that the time required for equilibrium to be established by diffusion alone is very great, and, of course, all mechanical disturbance of the liquid must be avoided in these experiments. The experiments were then repeated, allowing the tubes to remain undisturbed for a much longer time. The result was that a larger difference was found between the concentrations of the warmer and colder solutions, for a given difference in temperature, than in the first series of experiments. Results were finally obtained which are very satisfactory, as the following examples will show:

The two portions of a solution of copper sulphate were kept at 20 degrees and 80 degrees, respectively. The change in concentration calculated from the law of Gay Lussac is 14.3 per cent; the difference in concentration found is 14.03 per cent. In another case, where the difference calculated was 24.8 per cent, the difference found was 23.87 per cent.

If the tubes had been allowed to remain still longer, it seems probable that the values found would have agreed even more closely with those calculated. The difference is, however, so small that the conclusion is justified that the *Law of Gay Lussac for Gas-pressure Applies to the Osmotic Pressure of Solutions.*

The applicability of the two laws of gas-pressure thus far considered to the osmotic pressure of solutions, simply shows that the two sets of phenomena are analogous, but tells us nothing as to the actual magnitude of the two pressures, or as to the relations between these magnitudes. We must now take another step and ascertain, if possible, what relation exists between the actual pressure exerted by a gas of given concentration and at a given temperature, and the osmotic pressure of a solution containing the same number of dissolved parts in a given volume as there are gas particles in the same volume; the osmotic pressure being, of course, measured at the same temperature as the gas-pressure.

Van't Hoff compared the gas-pressure of hydrogen gas, with the osmotic pressure of a solution of cane sugar of the same concentration as the gas; i. e., having the same number of sugar molecules in a given volume of the solution as there are hydrogen molecules in the same volume of the gas. The result, which is very surprising, is that, *the solution exerted an osmotic press- ure which was exactly equal to the gas- pressure exerted by the gas, and since the Law of Avogadro Applies to Gases, It Must, therefore, Apply to Solutions.*

The law of Avogadro, as applied to gases, states that equal volumes of all gases at the same temperature and pressure contain the same number of ultimate parts. As applied to solutions it would be formulated thus; equal volumes of all solutions, which, at the same temperature have the same osmotic pressure, contain the same number of ultimate parts.

We have thus far seen that the three fundamental laws of gas-pressure apply to the osmotic pressure of solutions;* but we know that there are conditions under which these laws do not hold for the pressures exerted by gases. If the gases are very concentrated, neither the law of Boyle nor that of Gay Lussac will apply to its pressure. The relations between gas-pressure and osmotic pressure are all the more striking, in that for the same conditions under which the laws do not apply to gases, they do not apply to the osmotic pressure of solutions. Although it is impossible to measure directly the osmotic pressure of concentrated solutions, there are a number of indirect methods of doing so; and from the results obtained by these indirect methods it is quite certain that neither the law of Boyle nor that of Gay Lussac applies to the osmotic pressure of concentrated solutions.

The relations between gas-pressure and osmotic pressure are certainly made very striking by the fact, that the three fundamental laws of gas-pressure apply to the osmotic pressure of solutions, but these relations are certainly made much closer, and become more interesting, when we learn that under exactly the same conditions which present exceptions to the laws of gas-pressure, we have exceptions manifesting themselves in the same sense, when we attempt to apply these laws to osmotic pressure.

SIGNIFICANCE OF THE ABOVE RELATIONS.

The full significance of the above relations between gas-pressure and osmotic pressure, could be appreciated only by one who has a comprehensive knowledge of the whole subject of modern physical chemistry. The importance of these relations in certain directions is, however, so obvious that it cannot fail to be recognized.

The fact that the osmotic pressure of solutions obeys the gas laws, makes it possible to deal with solutions in many respects as we deal with gases. Before these relations were known, the whole subject of solutions seemed to be of secondary interest and importance. It was recognized, to be sure, that most chemical reactions take place in solution, but there was no efficient means of dealing with solutions as such. Any one who is at all familiar with the principles of physics, knows full well that matter in the gaseous state lends itself to our methods of investigation, and especially to mathematical methods, better than in any other form of aggregation. We can readily apply thermodynamics to gases, and it may be said in general that we know far more about matter in the condition of a gas than in the condition of a liquid; and, in turn, far more about the liquid condition than about the solid. Indeed, our knowledge of matter in the solid state, other than its external form, is, after

---

* For a fuller discussion of this subject, with thermodynamic demonstrations, see Van't Hoff's original paper (*Loc. cit.*) or Theory of Electrolytic Dissociation—Jones.

all, very superficial and most unsatisfactory.

Since we can deal with gases mathematically, and since the laws of gas-pressure apply to the osmotic pressure of solutions, we can apply mathematics to solutions in a manner analogous to that which has been used with gases. The result is that the very greatest advances have been made in the study of solutions, since the relations described in this paper were pointed out by Van't Hoff in 1887. Since we can deal with solutions by entirely new methods, and since solutions lie at the basis of most chemical phenomena, we have new methods opened up for dealing with these phenomena.

The importance of these relations for the subject in hand cannot easily be over-estimated, as we shall probably see before this series of papers is concluded. Their influence is felt throughout a large portion of the field of electrochemistry, and some of the most important developments in electrochemistry in the last fifteen years have been based directly upon them. To take one example, the action of the primary cell. This was not understood and not satisfactorily explained until these relations were discovered. It was not even known where the chief source of the electromotive force was. We can now explain the action of the primary cell in a satisfactory manner, and can go even farther and calculate the electromotive force; into this calculation, as we shall see, the osmotic pressures of the solutions around the electrodes entering and playing a prominent rôle. In the modern developments in electrochemistry, this wide-reaching generalization connecting osmotic pressure and gas-pressure is not the only factor. Another generalization of even greater importance is involved, and to this we shall turn in the next chapter.

CHAPTER II—THE THEORY OF ELECTROLYTIC DISSOCIATION.

IN THE PRECEDING chapter we saw how osmotic pressure was shown to obey the same laws as gas-pressure, and how Van't Hoff arrived at this generalization, which is one of the most important in modern chemical science.

The conclusion would be drawn from what has been said thus far, that the osmotic pressure of all substances conforms to the gas laws. Such is not the case by any means. Indeed, there are a great many exceptions to this law, and, as so frequently happens, the exceptions are as interesting, or even of greater interest, than the cases which conform to rule.

If we were to study the osmotic pressures exerted by all known substances, we would find that certain classes of compounds exert an *osmotic pressure which was much greater* than that exerted by other classes of substances. Indeed, chemical compounds would divide themselves into two great classes, according to the magnitude of the osmotic pressure which they would exert. The one class would show a pressure which conforms to the gas laws, and which we call normal; the other a pressure which, in some cases was twice, in others three times as great. In the former class we should find all those substances like cane sugar, the alcohols, aldehydes, ethers, ketones, etc.; in general, the chemically inactive substances. In the other class we would have the acids, bases, and salts; or, in general, those substances which are chemically most active.

A closer examination of the two classes would show that in the former occur all those substances which, when dissolved in water, do not conduct the electric current, and only those; or, in a word, the *non-electrolytes*. In the latter we have all those compounds which, when dissolved in water, conduct the current, and only those, and hence are known as the *electrolytes*.

Van't Hoff recognized clearly these two great classes of substances, which differed widely from one another with respect to the magnitude of the osmotic pressure which they could exert. In the paper to which reference has already been frequently made, he pointed out that many anomalies exist when we try to apply the gas laws to the osmotic pressures of solutions of substances in general; and stated clearly that "examples in aqueous solutions are most of the salts, the strong acids, and the strong bases."

Van't Hoff was not able to offer a satisfactory explanation of why the non-electrolytes give osmotic pressures which conform to the gas laws, while electrolytes all exert greater osmotic pressures. This was reserved for another.

ORIGIN OF THE THEORY OF ELECTROLYTIC DISSOCIATION.

The Swedish physicist, Arrhenius, who at that time was working with Ostwald in Leipzig, became interested in the great differences which manifested themselves between non-electrolytes and electrolytes, and especially in the work of, and conclusions reached by, Van't Hoff. Arrhenius pointed out that non-electrolytes differ from electrolytes not only in the osmotic pressures which they exert, but in certain other properties.

It is well known that when a substance is dissolved in a solvent, the freezing-point of the latter is lowered; the solution freezing lower than the pure solvent. This is well exemplified in nature in the case of sea-water, which freezes lower than pure water. The work of the French chemist, Raoult,* had shown that the lowering of tne freezing-point of water produced by non-electrolytes depended only upon the ratio between the number of molecules of the solvent and those of the dissolved substance; i. e., upon the concentration of the solution. Any non-electrolyte lowered the freezing-point of water to just the same extent as any other non-electrolyte of comparable concentration, and by comparable concentration is meant the same number of molecules of the dissolved substance in a given volume of the solution.

A molecule of any non-electrolyte produced just the same lowering of the freezing-point of a given number of molecules of water, as a molecule of any other non-electrolyte.

The electrolytes, however, behave very differently with respect to their power to lower the freezing-point of a solvent. *The lowering produced by them was always greater* than that produced by the non-electrolytes. Here we have results similar to those obtained from a study of the osmotic pressures of electrolytes and non-electrolytes. The former exert a greater osmotic pressure, and produce a greater lowering of the freezing point of the solvent than the latter. The agreement be-

tween the two sets of phenomena is more than qualitative. We have seen that the electrolytes exert twice, and in some cases three times the osmotic pressure of non-electrolytes of comparable concentrations. So, here, we find that the electrolytes lower the freezing-point of water twice, and in some cases three times as much as the non-electrolytes of comparable concentrations.

The analogies between the properties of the two great classes of chemical compounds are not yet exhausted. It is well known that the presence of a dissolved substance lowers the vapor-tension of the solvent. Raoult also showed that non-electrolytes produce the same lowering of the vapor-tension of a solvent, if they are present at the same molecular concentration, regardless of the nature of the non-electrolyte. Electrolytes, on the other hand, always produce greater lowering of the vapor-tension than non-electrolytes, and, again, in some cases twice the lowering, and in other cases three times the lowering.

These were some of the facts which had to be dealt with by any theory which would account for the difference between non-electrolytes and electrolytes in solution in water. It is obvious from what has been said that all three of the properties considered—osmotic pressure, lowering of freezing point, and lowering of vapor-tension—are properties which depend upon numbers only; the magnitude of each and all of them depending, as we have seen, only upon the ratio between the number of molecules of the dissolved substance and the number of molecules of the solvent. If these phenomena depend only upon numbers, and if they have a magnitude greater than would be expected,

* Raoult was Professor of Chemistry at Grenoble France, where he died a few months ago.

the only conclusion is that *there are a larger number of parts present than we would expect.*

This is essentially the way the problem presented itself to Arrhenius. We seem, then, forced to the conclusion that in solutions of electrolytes (acids, bases, and salts) we have more parts present than would correspond to the molecules of the respective substances. The question naturally arose, how is this possible? A molecule is the simplest unit of a compound of which we can conceive, and yet we must have particles in solution which are more numerous than the molecules. The inevitable conclusion is that the molecules themselves must be broken down into parts. But the difficulty was by no means as yet overcome. How could we conceive of the molecules of such substances as hydrochloric acid, potassium hydroxide, or potassium chloride, breaking down in the presence of water into simpler parts? If a substance like potassium chloride should break down into potassium and chlorine, the potassium would act on water with its well-known vigor, giving potassium hydroxide and hydrogen gas. We know, however, that this is not the case. Potassium chloride dissolved in water does not act chemically at all upon the water; the only change produced being a slight change in temperature, due to the solid passing into solution. We thus seem to be in a hopeless dilemma; phenomena such as we have been considering demanding that the molecules of electrolytes break down in solution, and the nature of electrolytes being such that it seems impossible that any such decompositions could take place.

Arrhenius, however, did not give the problem up, as men less earnest might

have done, but went to the literature to see what suggestions had already been made to account for the condition of acids, bases, and salts in solution. He found that Williamson had proposed a theory in 1851 to account for the synthesis of ordinary ether from sulphuric acid and alcohol, which stated that in solution the molecules were broken down more or less completely into their constituents, which then recombined forming new molecules. In solution there was, then, a continual interchange of parts going on—a succession of decompositions and recombinations. This did not assist Arrhenius very much, since it left unanswered the question, why do not the parts (say potassium) act chemically upon the solvent water? He was, however, more successful when he turned to a theory which had been proposed in 1856 by Clausius, to account for the fact that a very weak current can decompose water. It had been shown that a current which was far too weak to decompose a molecule of water, can effect the electrolysis of water to which a small amount of an electrolyte had been added. If the current could not decompose one molecule of water it is obvious that it could not decompose more than one, and yet it caused an appreciable amount of hydrogen to be set free at one pole, and of oxygen at the other pole. To account for this and similar facts, Clausius assumed that some few of the molecules of water are already decomposed before the current is passed—decomposed not into atoms, but into atoms which were charged with electricity— the one positive and the other negative, and called *ions*. *An ion is, therefore, a charged atom or group of atoms.*

This gave Arrhenius the clue to the explanation of such phenomena as we have been considering. The electrolytes gave abnormally large osmotic pressure, abnormally great depression of the freezing-point, and abnormally great depression of the vapor-tension of the solvent, because their molecules were broken down into ions. The ions being atoms or groups of atoms charged with electricity, differed fundamentally in properties from the same atoms or groups when uncharged; and, consequently, the difficulty that substances like potassium chloride could not break down into their constituents in the presence of water, because potassium in the atomic or molecular condition acts so vigorously upon water, was overcome. The ion of potassium has, necessarily, no property in common with the atom of potassium, except that of mass, which remains unchanged when the atom becomes an ion. *Thus arose the theory of electrolytic dissociation,* in the hands of Arrhenius.

It might, however, be concluded from what has been said, that Arrhenius did nothing more than take the suggestion which had been made by Clausius and apply it to these newly discovered phenomena, but such is not the case. The suggestion which had been made by Clausius was purely qualitative. It simply stated that in water there are a *few* molecules broken down into ions. It did not say what percentage of the molecules is broken down into ions, and Clausius did not point out any method by which this could be determined.

Arrhenius took this purely qualitative suggestion of Clausius and converted it into a quantitative theory, by pointing out methods by which the amount of dissociation could be measured. If the theory was true, the amount of dissociation as measured by the different methods, must

agree. If different methods gave different results, it would be a very strong argument against the correctness of the theory of electrolytic dissociation. We shall turn now to this phase of the problem.

TESTING THE THEORY OF ELECTROLYTIC DISSOCIATION.

In his original paper,[*] which has now become a classic, Arrhenius not only proposed the theory of electrolytic dissociation, but pointed out methods by which its truth could be tested. If this is to become a general theory of solution, it must not only account for the abnormally large osmotic pressure exerted by electrolytes, but also for the abnormally large freezing-point lowering, and lowering of vapor-tension produced by these substances. If we reverse the line of reasoning and measure the amount of dissociation by the abnormally large osmotic pressure exerted by the electrolytes, we should obtain exactly the same result as when we measured the dissociation by the abnormally large lowering of freezing-point, or abnormally large lowering of vapor-tension produced by these substances. Arrhenius applied just this test to his theory. He measured dissociation, on the one hand, by the lowering of freezing-point produced, and, on the other, by the osmotic pressure which was exerted by the electrolytes, and compared the two sets of values obtained.

This matter is of such great historical importance in connection with the development of the whole theory of electrolytic dissociation, that it must be considered in some detail. The fundamental principle underlying the deduction of Arrhenius is that an ion exerts exactly the

[*] On the Dissociation of Substances Dissolved in Water. *Ztschr. phys Chem* I. 631. Translated into English by H C Jones. *Science Memoir Series.* iv. p 47. (Amer. Book Co.)

same osmotic pressure as a molecule, and produces the same lowering of the freezing-point and of the vapor-tension of a solvent as a molecule. This follows from the fact, which has already been pointed out, that these phenomena depend only upon numbers, and since ions are independent individuals, their influence on the properties is exactly the same as molecules.

Since we can deal with ions and molecules indiscriminately in connection with these properties, the calculation of the percentage dissociation by means of osmotic pressure or freezing-point lowering becomes very simple. Suppose we are dealing with a binary electrolyte; *i. e.,* with one which dissociates into two ions. If it is not dissociated at all it will exert the same osmotic pressure, and produce the same lowering of the freezing-point as a non-electrolyte of the same concentration. If it is completely dissociated it will produce twice this osmotic pressure and lowering of freezing-point. If it is partly dissociated it will produce an osmotic pressure and lowering of freezing-point which lies somewhere between these values. By simple proportion, then, we obtain at once the amount of dissociation, knowing the osmotic pressure or the lowering of the freezing-point exerted by the substance.

Arrhenius proceeded as follows: The lowering of the freezing-point of water produced by a gram-molecular weight of a non-electrolyte in a litre of solution is 1°.86. Such a solution is, of course, a normal solution, as this expression is used in chemistry; and the quantity, 1°.86, is known as the molecular lowering of the freezing-point of water, or the freezing-point constant of water. If the freezing-

point lowering actually observed for the electrolyte of normal concentration is t°, the ratio between these two does not give the dissociation, but gives a coefficient i; which, from its discoverer, has come to be known as the Van't Hoff i. From the freezing-point lowering then, $i = \dfrac{t°}{1°.86}$. The dissociation a is obtained at once from the coefficient i. For a binary electrolyte $a = i - 1$; for a ternary electrolyte, $a = \dfrac{i - 1}{2}$.

Arrhenius then calculated the value of i from osmotic pressure, as follows: If we represent by m the number of undissociated molecules present, by n the number of dissociated molecules, and by k the number of ions into which each molecule dissociates, we have

$$i = \frac{m + kn}{m + n}.$$

The values of i were thus calculated by two entirely different methods; it now remained to see whether the two sets of values agreed with each other, or whether they did not. If there was an agreement it was a strong argument in favor of the correctness of the new theory; if there was not an agreement it would be unfortunate for the theory. A very few* of the results which were obtained by Arrhenius for acids, bases, and salts, are given below:

ACIDS.

	i from Freezing Point Lowering.	i from Osmotic Pressure.
Hydrochloric acid....	1.98	1.
Nitric "	1.94	1.
Sulphuric "	2.06	3
Formic " ...	1.04	1.90
Malic "	1.08	1.98

* For a fuller discussion of this subject with the results which were obtained, see Theory of Electrolytic Dissociation (H. C. Jones), pp. 96–100.

BASES.

	i from Freezing Point Lowering.	i from Osmotic Pressure.
Potassium hydroxide.	1.91	1.93
Sodium "	1.96	1.88
Barium "	2.69	2.67
Calcium "	2.59	2.59
Ammonium "	1.03	1.01

SALTS.

Potassium chloride....	1.82	1.85
Sodium " ...	1.90	1.82
Ammonium "	1.88	1.84
Sodium nitrate........	1.82	1.82
Potassium acetate....	1.86	1.83
Sodium carbonate ..	2.18	2.22
Strontium nitrate. ...	2.23	2.23
Lead nitrate..........	2.02	2.08
Cupric acetate........	1.68	1.66

These comparisons were made for about 15 bases, 23 acids, and 40 salts, and while some apparent discrepancies, appeared, still, an unmistakeable agreement existed between the two sets of values.

Almost as quickly as these agreements were pointed out for so many electrolytes, the theory began to attract attention. Here were facts which, from their nature, could not be disregarded, and from their number could not be referred to accident. There must be a large element of truth in any generalization which accords so well with so much experimental data. This seems to be about the way in which the whole subject presented itself to the more progressive men, some 14 years ago when the paper by Arrhenius appeared. They saw in this theory a generalization which was capable of accounting for a large number of facts which, before it was proposed, were entirely inexplicable in terms of any conception known at that time.

The theory of electrolytic dissociation, like all wide-reaching generalizations, was fortunate in that it did not escape criticism from conservative hands. I do not refer to that kind of criticism which is based upon a lack of familiarity with the facts involved, and which was poured out in abundance against this theory for a time from certain quarters; but to legitimate criticism, based upon real difficulties encountered when an honest attempt was made to apply it to certain classes of facts—a criticism based upon an earnest desire to arrive at the truth. I have referred to this kind of criticism as fortunate, since it puts a theory upon its mettle, as it were, and sifts the wheat from the chaff. If the theory has any value it will be brought out, or, if it is inherently incapable and worthless, it will be overthrown before it has done any harm to the advance of science. It was such criticism as this that made the supporters of the new view look around for evidence bearing upon it. A few of the many lines of evidence bearing upon the theory of electrolytic dissociation will now be taken up.

FURTHER LINES OF EVIDENCE* BEARING UPON THE THEORY OF ELEC-
LYTIC DISSOCIATION.

The theory of electrolytic dissociation says that acids, bases, and salts in the presence of water are broken down into their ions, the amount of the dissociation of any compound depending chiefly upon the concentration of the solution. As the dilution increases the percentage dissociation increases, until at a dilution of about 1,000 litres,† the strong acids and bases, and the salts in general, are completely dissociated. These substances, at this dilution, exist, then, only in the ionic condition, there being no molecules present.

---

*The few lines of evidence for this theory, which will be considered in the remainder of this chapter, are discussed more fully and many other lines are taken up in my book, to which reference has already been made. Theory of Electrolytic Dissociation. (Macmillan's.)

† This means a solution which contains a gram-molecular weight of the electrolyte in 1,000 litres of the solution.

It is obvious that the properties of such solutions of these substances must be the properties of the ions present, and not those of the molecules, since there are no molecules in the solution. This applies to all the properties of such solutions, both physical and chemical. We have in this fact a means of testing the correctness of our theory, as we shall now see.

Let us take up certain properties of completely dissociated solutions, and see whether they are additive; *i. e.*, the sum of the corresponding properties of the ions which are present. We shall consider first the *specific gravity of solutions of certain salts.**

"If a salt is added to water, the volume of the solution is different from that of the pure solvent, and also from the sum of the volumes of the liquid and of the solid. If the resulting solution is very dilute, the salt is completely dissociated into its ions. Nernst has shown from the results of J. Traube, that the change in volume, under such conditions, is an additive property of the ions. Given a solution containing a gram-molecular weight of a salt whose molecular weight is M, in m grams of water. Let the specific gravity of the solution be S, the specific gravity of water s. *The change in volume* Δv. on dissolving the salt, will be :

$$\Delta v = \frac{M + m}{S} - \frac{m}{s}.$$

"The following results are given :

KC = 26.7		NaCl = 17.7	
KBr = 35.1		NaBr = 26.7	
KI = 45 4		NaI = 36.1	

$$\left. \begin{array}{l} KB\cdot - KCl = 8.4 \\ NaBr - NaCl = 9.0 \end{array} \right\} \qquad \left. \begin{array}{l} KI - KBr = 10.2 \\ NaI - NaBr = 9.4 \end{array} \right\}$$

$$\left. \begin{array}{l} KI - KCl = 18.7 \\ NaI - NaCl = 18 4 \end{array} \right\} \qquad \left\{ \begin{array}{l} KCl - NaCl = 9.0 \\ KBr - NaBr = 8.4 \\ KI - NaI = 9.3 \end{array} \right\}$$

"These results show the additive nature of the specific gravity of salt solutions. The difference between the chlorine and the bromine ions is about 8.7; between chlorine and iodine, 18.5; between bromine and iodine, 9.8; while between potassium and sodium it is about 9.0.

"The additive nature of the specific gravity of salt solutions had, indeed, been pointed out much earlier by Valson. He had shown exactly what is brought out above: Given salt solutions of comparable concentration; *i. e.*, containing, say, a gram-molecule of the salt per litre; the difference between the specific gravities of solutions containing two metals combined with the same acid is constant, whatever the nature of the acid. Similarly, the difference between the specific gravities of two salts of the same acid with any metal is constant, regardless of the nature of the metal. The specific gravity of a salt solution is then obtained by adding to a constant number two values—the one for the acid, the other for the metal. These values Valson termed 'moduli'; and he worked out their values for a large number of elements.

"Valson concluded from his work that the molecules of salts must be completely broken down in solution. But the evidence in favor of such a view was not strong enough at that time to bring it into favor."

One other property of solutions of salts will be considered in this connection, that it may be seen that the above relations are not merely accidental. When acids and bases neutralize one another, a change in volume is produced. If a litre of a normal solution of a univalent acid is brought together with a litre of a normal solution of a univalent base, the result-

---

* This paragraph is quoted from the Theory of Electrolytic Dissociation. p. 105.

ing volume is not two litres, but somewhat less, there being, in general, a contraction in volume.*

"The change of volume produced by neutralizing acids with bases has been extensively studied by Ostwald. The solutions contained a gram-equivalent of the acid or base, in a kilogram, and were, therefore, not completely dissociated; so that if the change in volume was additive, it would be shown only approximately by such solutions.

"Ostwald worked with 19 acids, including the strongest mineral acids, and some of the more strongly dissociated organic acids. He neutralized these with the three bases, potassium, sodium and ammonium. A few of his results are given, the change in volume being expressed in cubic centimetres. The differences in the horizontal lines are the differences between potassium, sodium, and ammonium, in combination with the same acid. The differences in the vertical columns are the differences between the different acids in combination with the same bases, obtained by subtracting the value for the acid from the value for nitric acid.

	Potassium Hydroxide.	Sodium Hydroxide.	Ammonium Hydroxide.
Nitric acid,	20.03 (0.28)	19.77 (26.91)	—6.44 (26.49)
	(0.55)	(0.53)	(0.15)
Hydrochloric acid,	19.58 (0.28)	19.94 (25.81)	—6.57 (26.09)
	(7.69)	(7.61)	(7.15)
Formic acid,	12.96 (0.20)	12.16 (25.75)	—13.59 (25.95)
	(10.55)	(10.49)	(9.88)
Acetic acid,	9.52 (0.24)	9.98 (25.54)	—16.26 (25.78)
	(8.15)	(8.29)	(7.91)
Sulphuric acid,	11.90 (0.42)	11.48 (25.63)	—14.35 (26.85)
	(11.82)	(11.84)	(11.19)
Succinic acid,	8.22 (0.80)	7.98 (25.56)	—17.68 (25.86)

" If we take the perpendicular rows in parentheses, we find very nearly a constant difference for the strong acids and bases. Similarly, if we take the horizontal rows in parentheses, we find very nearly a constant difference. This means that the difference in change of volume, produced by neutralizing two different bases by a given acid, is a constant, independent of the nature of the acid; and, similarly, the difference of the change in volume on neutralizing two different acids by a given base is independent of the nature of the base.

"The change in volume, when acids and bases neutralize each other, like the specific gravity of salt solutions, is, then, an additive property, depending both upon the nature of the acid and of the base; and we could work out here, as Valson has done in the case of specific gravities, the numerical values of the constants for each constituent."

A number of other physical properties of solutions of completely dissociated substances have been studied in a manner analogous to the above, with the result that they have been shown, in general, to be the sum of two constants, the one depending upon one ion, and the other upon the other ion. We should mention, especially, the *color of solutions* of completely dissociated substances. Ostwald has carried out an elaborate study of this property of solutions of about 300 colored substances. Only a few of his results will be considered here, and we will take up one of the best known and simplest cases—the permanganates. The permanganates all dissociate in a manner analogous to potassium permanganate:

$$KMnO_4 = K + MnO_4.$$

The potassium ion is not colored, since it exists in solutions of potassium chloride, nitrate, sulphate, etc., and these solutions are colorless. The color of such solutions

---

must be due, then, entirely to the presence of the MnO_4 ion.

This same line of reasoning holds for all permanganates in which the metal is colorless. The color of the solutions of these salts must be due entirely to the presence of the ion of permanganic acid, MnO_4. The conclusion is that the color of solutions of all the permanganates, in which the metal is colorless, must be the same. This was studied by Ostwald, who determined the absorption spectra of solutions of ten or a dozen such permanganates, and found that the absorption bands of all of them fell at exactly the same places in the spectroscope. The positions of these bands were measured, and they were also photographed and compared by superposition. The general result was just what would be expected if our theory were true—the colors of the different permanganates are exactly the same; and further, the same as that of permanganic acid which dissociates into MnO_4 and hydrogen, and the latter ion is known to be colorless since solutions of acids like hydrochloric, nitric, sulphuric, etc., in which an abundance of hydrogen ions are present, are colorless.

The conclusion from the study of the color of solutions, like that from the study of other physical properties, is in perfect accord with the theory of electrolytic dissociation, and it is very difficult to see how these facts could be interpreted if this generalization had not been reached.

Evidence has been obtained for the correctness of the theory of electrolytic dissociation from a study of the *properties* of *mixtures* of substances. We shall take first a mixture of substances which are readily dissociated, and then a mixture of substances which are not dissociated at all. Let us take a mixture of potassium nitrate and sodium iodide, and make a very dilute solution of the mixture. Since both salts are readily dissociated at moderate dilutions, we would have them both completely broken down into their ions, thus:

$$K + NO_3 + Na + I.$$

The properties of the mixture, both chemical and physical, would be the sum of the properties of these four ions.

If now we mix potassium iodide and sodium nitrate and make a dilute solution of the mixture, we would have both salts completely dissociated into their ions, which would be:

$$K + I + Na + NO_3.$$

In terms of our theory, we would have exactly the same ions in the two cases, and the properties of the two mixtures should be identical. Such is the fact. The two mixtures referred to above, using equivalent quantities of the different substances, are, in every respect, identical.

If, on the other hand, we mix two substances which are not dissociated to any appreciable extent by water, and dissolve the mixture, we would have different solutions, according to the theory, depending upon which substances were combined at the outset. Thus, a mixture of methyl alcohol and ethyl chloride would have properties which were the sum of the properties of the molecules CH_3OH and C_2H_5Cl. The properties of a mixture of ethyl alcohol and methyl chloride would be the sum of the properties of the molecules C_2H_5OH and CH_3Cl. Since, in the two mixtures the molecules are different, the properties of the two mixtures should be different. Here, again, facts and theory are in perfect agreement. The two mixtures have very different properties.

It is not easy to lay too much stress upon these facts as bearing upon the general correctness of the theory of electrolytic dissociation. Without this theory such facts would be entirely inexplicable; with it they are just what we would expect. One could scarcely wish for stronger arguments in favor of the general truth of the theory of electrolytic dissociation.

AN EXPERIMENTAL DEMONSTRATION OF DISSOCIATION.

This chapter should not be concluded without reference to a very simple experiment, which demonstrates to the eye the dissociating action of a solvent like water. If a few drops of an alcoholic solution of phenolphthaleïn are added to a cylinder containing, say, 100 c.c. of alcohol, and a drop of aqueous ammonia added and the cylinder shaken, there will be no trace of the purple color which is characteristic of this indicator in the presence of alkalies. If, now, water is added to the alcohol, the purple color will begin to appear, and will become deeper and deeper as more and more water is added.

The explanation of what takes place is comparatively simple. Ammonia is a base which is dissociated only slightly, even by so strong a dissociating agent as water. By alcohol it is scarcely dissociated at all. In order that a base may react with phenolphthaleïn it must be dissociated to some extent. Ammonia in alcohol does not react alkaline with phenolphthaleïn, because it is not sufficiently dissociated. If, now, water is added, this dissociates the ammonia, and we have our indicator showing its characteristic alkaline reaction. If more alcohol is added the dissociation of the ammonia is driven back, as we say, and the color disappears.

We have thus a demonstration to the eye of the dissociating action of water, expressing itself in the color of the phenolphthaleïn.

This demonstration becomes still more instructive if we carry out in addition the following experiment. Let us proceed exactly as described above, using a drop of an aqueous solution of potassium hydroxide instead of ammonium hydroxide. As soon as the potassium hydroxide is added to the alcohol containing phenolphthalïn, the purple color appears without the addition of water. This fact was also predicted by us[*] from the theory before the experiment was tried. Potassium hydroxide is a strongly dissociated base, and is sufficiently dissociated even by alcohol to show the alkaline reaction with phenolphthaleïn.[†]

We have thus presented a very little of the enormous mass of evidence bearing upon the theory of electrolytic dissociation. While certain facts are known which have given some difficulty when an attempt was made to fit them in with the theory, the great preponderance of evidences points to its general correctness. It should be said that as experimental work is more and more carefully done, the number of apparent exceptions to the theory becomes rather less than more; so that while we should always welcome real exceptions to the theory, we should not be in too great a hurry to accept apparent discrepancies until they have been thoroughly tested by experiment.[‡]

Accepting the theory of electrolytic dissociation as a most fruitful working hypothesis, we shall consider in the next chapter some applications which have been made of it.

---

[*] Jones and Allu; *American Chemical Journal,* xviii, 377.

[†] For a fuller explanation of this experiment, see Theory of Electrolytic Dissociation. pp 113–115.

[‡] An account of some apparent exceptions, which have been shown to be due entirely to experimental error, will soon be published in the *American Chemical Journal.*

CHAPTER III—SOME APPLICATIONS OF THE THEORY OF ELECTROLYTIC DISSOCIATION.

HAVING TRACED in the preceding chapter how the theory of electrolytic dissociation arose, and a few lines of evidence pointing to the conclusion that it expresses a great truth, we must now ask of what service the theory has been. Has it pointed out methods of dealing with new problems, or has it furnished us with new methods of dealing with old problems? Has it suggested new lines of investigation, or has it been able to correlate facts which were apparently disconnected? If it has accomplished any one of these things it is valuable; if it has accomplished more than one, so much the greater its value.

In this chapter we shall aim to show how the theory of electrolytic dissociation has been applied to a few problems, mainly of a chemical nature, and what is the character of the results obtained.

THE NEUTRALIZATION OF ACIDS AND BASES.

A chemical reaction which is about as familiar as any other, is the neutralization of an acid by a base. It has long been known that whenever an acid and a base are brought together, each neutralizes the other and a salt is formed. The process of neutralization was looked upon as a special act for each acid and each base, the nature of the process depending upon the nature of the acid used and upon the nature of the base used. It was recognized, to be sure, that in the neutralization of acids by bases water is always formed, but this was regarded as of secondary impor-

tance. The formation of the salt was the important feature, and this was different for each acid or each base employed. The result of the study of neutralization was, then, the collection of a great mass of more or less disconnected details, between which no very close relations were recognized.

Since the theory of electrolytic dissociation was proposed, we regard the whole process of neutralization in an entirely different light. An acid is represented by the general expression,

$$\mathrm{RH} = \bar{\mathrm{R}} + \overset{+}{\mathrm{H}},$$

where R is the negative ion (anion) and differs for every acid, the positive ion (cation) hydrogen is the same for every acid, and is the constituent which is essential to acidity. Whenever we have an acid in the presence of a dissociating solvent like water, we have hydrogen ions formed, and, conversely, whenever we have hydrogen ions present we have acidity. A base, in terms of our theory, is to be represented thus:

$$\mathrm{R'OH} = \overset{+}{\mathrm{R}'} + \overset{-}{\mathrm{OH}},$$

R' being the cation of the base, which differs for every base employed, and the anion, $\overline{\mathrm{OH}}$, is common to all bases. Wherever we have a base in the presence of water we have hydroxyl ions, and the converse is also true, that wherever we have hydroxyl ions we have basic properties.

What takes place, in terms of our theory, when an acid is brought in contact with a base? The anion of the acid, which, as we have seen, varies from acid to acid, and the cation of the base, which is the variable quality for the base, remain in exactly the same condition after the acid and base are brought into contact as before. The only act which takes place is the union of the hydrogen ion of the acid with the hydroxyl ion of the base, forming a molecule of water. These facts would

$$\overset{-}{R} + \overset{+}{H} + \overset{-}{OH} + \overset{+}{R'} \quad R + \overset{+}{R'} + H_2O.$$

This is very simple, but the fundamental question still remains, is it true? At first sight it appears that it cannot be true, because we know that when an acid is neutralized by a base, a salt is formed. The above statements and the formula do not take into account at all the formation of any salt. How is this apparent discrepancy to be accounted for? It is accounted for very readily on the ground that our earlier conceptions of the formation of salts from the action of acids on bases are in error. When a dilute solution of an acid acts on a dilute solution of a base, there is not the slightest reason for supposing that any salt whatever is formed; and we are dealing with dilute solutions of both compounds in order that both may be completely dissociated. It is true that we obtain a salt from the mixture of an acid with a base, by evaporation; but this does not prove, and, indeed, is not the slightest reason for supposing, that a salt exists as such in the dilute solution of the mixture. Indeed, if we take the very salt which is obtained by evaporating the mixture of the acid and base, and prepare a dilute solution of it, the solution will contain no molecules whatever of the salt, but only the ions into which the molecules have dissociated.

This alone would show that the old conception of neutralization must be in error, and is a strong argument in favor of the general correctness of the view expressed by the above equation.

We must, however, analyze the above conception more closely. According to the new view, all that takes place in the neutralization of an acid by a base, is the union of the hydrogen ion of the acid with the hydroxyl ion of the base. This assumes, of course, that hydrogen and hydroxyl ions in the presence of one another do combine. If we look around for experimental confirmation of this assumption, we find an abundance of it. Space will not permit of a discussion of these experiments, but there are no less than six or seven separate and independent lines of investigation, every one of which has shown that hydrogen and hydroxyl ions cannot exist in the presence of each other to any appreciable extent uncombined. Experiment and theory are thus in perfect accord on this point.

Since the process of neutralization consists in nothing but the union of the hydrogen ions of the acid with the hydroxyl ions of the base, then, one process of neutralization is exactly the same as any other—the neutralization of any acid by any base is exactly the same as the neutralization of any other acid by any other base. This point can also be tested experimentally. If all processes of neutralization are the same, consisting in the formation of molecule of water, then the heat which is liberated when an equivalent of an acid acts on an equivalent of a base, must be the same as the heat set free when an equivalent of any other acid acts on an equivalent of the same or any other base. This conclusion is beautifully confirmed by experiment. It has long been known that the heat which is liberated when a dilute solution of a strong acid acts on a dilute solution of a strong base, is a constant, independent of the nature of the acid, and independent of the nature of the base. This will be seen from the following results:

HEAT OF NEUTRALIZATION.

$$HCl \ + NaOH = 13,700 \text{ cal.}$$
$$HBr \ + NaOH = 13,700 \text{ cal.}$$
$$HNO_3 + NaOH = 13,700 \text{ cal.}$$

Varying the nature of the base and keeping the acid constant, we have:

$$HCl + LiOH \qquad\quad = 13,700 \text{ cal.}$$
$$HCl + KOH \qquad\quad = 13,700 \text{ cal.}$$
$$HCl + \tfrac{1}{2} Ba\,(OH)_2 = 13,800 \text{ cal.}$$
$$HCl + \tfrac{1}{2} Ca\,(OH)_2 = 13,900 \text{ cal.}$$

The thermal measurements furnish a beautiful confirmation of the theory, being constant, independent of the nature of the acid, and independent of the nature of the base, to within the limits of experimental error.

The story is, however, not yet complete. Suppose that either the acid or the base is not completely dissociated, and still more, that both are incompletely dissociated, what would take place in terms of our theory in these cases?

If either the acid or base is not completely dissociated, then, as the ions already present are used up, more and more of the undissociated molecules will break down into ions, until the dissociation has proceeded to the limit and the neutralization is complete. The dissociation of the originally undissociated molecules, however, is accompanied by thermal change, heat being usually liberated as dissociation proceeds, but in some few cases heat is absorbed. The heat of neutralization would, therefore, be accompanied by the heat of ionization of the compounds in question, and the heat of ionization varies with every compound used.

In such cases, then, where either the acid or base is incompletely dissociated (and still more where both are incompletely dissociated), the heat which is set free when the two are brought together is not simply the heat of neutralization, but this plus the heat of ionization, which is usually a positive quantity.

If we neutralize a weak* acid with a weak base, our theory would lead us to conclude that the heat set free would not be a constant for different substances, but would vary both with the nature of the acid and the nature of the base.

And since the heat of ionization is usually positive, it would lead to the conclusion that the heat of neutralization of weak acids and bases would generally be greater than that set free when strong† acids are neutralized by strong bases. The following facts confirm very beautifully the conclusion from the theory.

HEAT OF NEUTRALIZATION.

$$HF + NaOH \qquad\qquad = 16,270 \text{ cal.}$$
$$H_3PO_4 + NaOH \qquad\quad = 14,830 \text{ cal.}$$
$$CHCl_2COOH‡ + NaOH = 14,830 \text{ cal.}$$

The theory of electrolytic dissociation, then, not only applies to the cases where the heats of neutralization are constant, but is equally applicable to those other cases where the heats of neutralization are not constant, and which would appear at first sight to present exceptions to the theory. Indeed, all of these facts are necessary consequences of our theory, and it would be unfortunate for the theory if they

---

* "Weak" acids or weak bases simply mean substances which are only slightly dissociated.
† "Strong" means great dissociation.
‡ Dichloracetic acid.

were not just what they have been found to be. We thus see how the theory of electrolytic dissociation accounts for all the facts which are known concerning the neutralization of acids and bases; but it has accomplished what is of far greater importance.

As has already been stated, before the theory was proposed each process of neutralization presented a new problem, depending upon the nature of the acid and the nature of the base used. It was recognized that water is always formed when acids and bases react, and it was supposed that there is some vital connection between all processes of neutralization; but what this was, was not perceived. The problem was rendered still more difficult by the supposed fact that in the process of neutralization a salt is formed, and this must be different for every acid and base which is used. Since a different product is obtained with each process of neutralization, it seemed impossible to refer all processes of neutralization to anything like a common cause.

We now know that all processes of neutralization of acids and bases are essentially the same, consisting only in the formation of a molecule of water. A more or less heterogeneous mass of facts is referred to a common cause, and thus correlated in a manner which would have been impossible without the theory of electrolytic dissociation. We shall learn that other great masses of facts have been dealt with in a similar manner, and generalizations reached through this great generalization, which are, in fact, but corollaries of it.

STRENGTH OF ACIDS AND BASES.

From the foot-notes to an earlier part of this paper, it would be gathered that there is a close relation between the "strength of compounds and the amounts of their dissociation. This subject is of such importance that it must be taken up more fully. Before the theory with which we are dealing came into vogue, the term "strength" was applied to chemical compounds in a more or less indefinite way. Various methods were adopted and used for determining the strengths of substances, and the results obtained depended largely upon the method which was employed. It was thought for a long time that of all the acids sulphuric is the strongest. This idea arose apparently from the fact that sulphuric acid is such a vigorous reagent on all forms of organic matter, and, further, because sulphuric acid readily replaces many other acids from their salts. This erroneous conclusion was, then, arrived at chiefly through a method which is not a sufficient test of the strengths of chemical compounds. This method is insufficient, chiefly because in the displacement of one acid from its salts by another acid, a number of factors come into play besides the relative strengths of the two acids. Thus, one of the compounds may be volatile and escape from the field of action as soon as it is formed, and this alone is sufficient to determine the direction and magnitude of the reaction; or one of the substances may be insoluble, and, as is well known, this is quite capable of conditioning the entire course of the reaction. As an example of the first case, take the action of sulphuric acid on chlorides of metals whose sulphates are soluble. We know that sulphuric acid can drive out practically all the hydrochloric acid from such compounds, the latter escaping from the field of action as a gas as rapidly as it is formed. Examples of insoluble compounds being formed and conditioning the entire course of the reaction, are so numerous that it may seem superfluous to select any one example. A whole class of illustrations is furnished by the action of the very weak acid, hydrogen sulphide, on the salts of strong acids with the heavy metals. Thus, hydrogen sulphide will precipitate copper, lead, mercury, etc., as sulphides, from their salts with the very strongest acids, such as hydrochloric and nitric. The number of illustrations of this principle is almost limitless; indeed, qualitative analysis in organic chemistry is made possible by, and based directly upon, this principle. Enough has, however, been said to show that the method involving the displacement of one substance from its compounds by another, is alone not a sufficient criterion of the relative strengths of the two substances.

A number of other methods have been devised and used for determining the relative strengths of substances, but these, like the above, are either insufficient in principle or are difficult to carry out in practice.

The theory of electrolytic dissociation has thrown entirely new light on this whole problem. The dissociation of the different acids has been worked out* on the one hand, and then their chemical activity, and the two sets of results have been compared. The following are a few of the results which have been obtained for some of the more common acids. In column I are given the dissociations of the acids referred to hydrochloric acid as 100; in column II the chemical activity of the acids, as measured by the velocity with which they are capable of effecting a certain reaction.

	I	II
Hydrochloric acid	100.0	100.0
Hydrobromic "	101.0	98.0
Nitric "	99.6	98.0
Sulphuric "	65.1	73.9
Acetic "	0.42	0.34
Monochloracetic acid	4.9	4.8
Dichloracetic "	25.3	23.0
Trichloracetic "	62.3	65.2
Oxalic "	19.7	17.6
Succinic "	0.84	0.50
Tartaric "	2.28	2.30

The agreement between the dissociations of the acids and their chemical activity is unmistakable.

The following are a few of the results which were obtained from some of the best known bases. Column I gives the dissociation, II the chemical activity:

	I	II
Potassium hydroxide	161.0	161.0
Sodium "	149.0	162.0
Ammonium "	4.06	8.0
Methylamine	20.02	19.0
Ethylamine	20.03	19.0
Dimethylamine	23.05	22.0
Trimethylamine	9.07	7.04
Tetrethylammonium hydroxide	128.0	131.0

Here, again, an unmistakable agreement exists.

To determine the relative strengths of compounds, at present, it is only necessary to measure their relative dissociations; but this is only a small part of the benefit to be derived from the theory in dealing with reactions in which these substances take part. Let us take some reaction which is effected by all acids, say, the inversion of cane sugar in the presence of water. This reaction takes place in the presence of hydrogen ions—the common constituents of all acids—as follows:

$$C_{12}H_{22}O_{11} + H_2O + \overset{+}{H} = C_6H_{12}O_6 +$$
$$C_6H_{12}O_6 + \overset{+}{H}$$

---

*One practical method of measuring dissociation was referred to in Chap. ii, based on the lowering of the freezing-point of solvents by dissolved substances. This will be considered more fully, and another method described in Chap. vi.

giving one molecule of dextrose and one of levulose.

The velocity with which this reaction will take place, other things being equal, depends upon the number of hydrogen ions present; *i. e.*, upon the dissociation of the acid. If we know the dissociations of different acids we can tell at once just how fast they would invert cane sugar, or accomplish any similar reaction; and, conversely, we can measure the dissociations of different acids by measuring the velocities with which they effect any given reaction like the above.

The remarks which have just been made concerning acids, apply with equal accuracy to bases. Take any reaction which is effected by the hydroxyl ion—the common ion of all bases—such as the saponification of an ester, which takes place in the sense of the following equation:

$$CH_3COOC_2H_5 + NaOH = C_2H_5OH + CH_3COONa.$$

The velocity with which this reaction will take place depends upon the number of hydroxyl ions present; *i. e.*, upon the dissociation of the base. If we know the dissociation of different bases we know the relative velocities with which they will effect the above reaction; and, conversely, if we know the relative velocities with which any given bases will effect the above reaction, we know their relative dissociations or strengths, since the two are proportional.

We can thus use dissociation to measure the chemical activities of substances, or we can use chemical activities to measure dissociation, since, as we have seen, a proportionality exists between the two.

CATALYTIC REACTIONS.

We cannot pass over the above reaction between cane sugar and water in the presence of acids, without making a slight digression from our general theme, to call attention to one peculiarity which exists. It will be observed that in the equation for this reaction, the hydrogen ion is written in the same condition on the two sides of the equation. This means that it does not enter as such into the reaction. If it does not enter into the reaction, why is its presence necessary in order that the reaction should take place with any appreciable velocity? We cannot at present answer this question, but it seems probable that the action of the hydrogen ion is a *surface action.* In the light of this conception it acts by contact, and such actions of substances, of which many are known, are termed *catalytic.* While we at present do not understand the mechanism of catalytic reactions, the problem is considerably simplified through the existence of the theory of electrolytic dissociation. Before this generalization had been proposed it was known that acids could effect certain catalytic reactions, but it was supposed that these reactions were produced by the whole molecules of the acids. We know now that the molecules of acids, as such, are not capable of producing catalytic reactions, but that it is the hydrogen ion into which the molecule dissociates, which acts catalytically—the anion of the acid taking no part whatever in the reaction.

The observations which have just been made in reference to the catalytic reactions of hydrogen ions, apply with equal force to the catalytic reactions of hydroxyl ions. The hydroxyl ions of bases can effect certain reactions catalytically, just as the hydrogen ions of acids, and the same rules which hold in the one case apply also in the other.*

COMPARISON OF REACTIONS BETWEEN IN-ORGANIC SUBSTANCES AND OR-GANIC SUBSTANCES.

It has long been known that inorganic substances in general have a much greater chemical activity than organic. This is shown very well in the relative velocities of the two sets of reactions. Inorganic reactions proceed so rapidly that in most cases it is impossible to measure their velocities. Indeed, their velocities are frequently so great, that they usually have been regarded as taking place instantaneously.

It is, however, quite different with organic reactions. They proceed, relatively, very much more slowly than inorganic, and in many cases their velocities are sufficiently small to enable them to be readily measured.

Why does this difference exist? A few years ago it would have been impossible to furnish a satisfactory answer to this question. It might have been said that inorganic reactions proceed more rapidly because the substances are chemically stronger, but this would have been simply renaming the phenomena, and not an explanation at all.

To-day we not only have a rational explanation of these facts in terms of our theory, but they are also a necessary consequence of it. Inorganic compounds are much more strongly dissociated than organic. Indeed, the inorganic acids and bases are the most strongly dissociated substances of which we have any knowledge,

and the salts are, as a class, among the most strongly dissociated substances. This applies to even the salts of the metals with weak acids, and the salts of strong acids with weak bases. Since chemical activity is proportional to dissociation, the most strongly dissociated substances must be the most active chemically.

Take the organic compounds, a great majority of them are dissociated very slightly, if at all; and even the organic acids and bases are among the weakly dissociated substances. The strongest of the organic acids is not as strong as sulphuric acid, which is only about three-fifths as strong as nitric or hydrochloric acid; while most of the organic acids are of the order of strength represented by acetic, malic, or tartaric acid; *i. e.,* scarcely more than a few hundredths of the strength of the strongest mineral acid. The same general remarks apply to the organic bases, though, perhaps, to not quite the same extent.

The organic compounds being, then, only slightly dissociated, react much more slowly than the inorganic; more ions being formed as the few already present are used up in the reaction, and this continuing until the end is reached, or more frequently until equilibrium is established between the velocities of the two opposite reactions.

Our theory furnishes us with a perfectly satisfactory explanation of all of these facts.

CHEMICAL ACTIVITY DUE TO IONS.

We have seen in the preceding paragraphs that chemical activity and dissociation are proportional to one another. If chemical activity is proportional to the number of ions present, then what part do the molecules play

---

* For some interesting cases of the catalytic action of finely divided metals, see recent work of Bredig and his pupils. *Ztschr. phys Chem.*, 1900-1901.

in chemical action? This question naturally forces itself upon us. To answer it we must, on the one hand, exclude molecules, and see whether ions react; and, on the other, we must exclude ions, and see whether molecules can react or not. To exclude molecules it is only necessary to prepare very dilute solutions of strong acids and bases, since in such solutions all the molecules are dissociated into ions. It has been seen that in *solutions which are completely dissociated,* taking into account the amount of substance present, the *chemical activity is a maximum.*

This would indicate either that ions alone can enter into chemical activity, or, at least, are much more active than molecules. To decide between these alternatives we must exclude ions altogether, and see whether molecules have any chemical activity. This can be accomplished by excluding all traces of moisture, and other solvents which have any dissociating power. The great experimental difficulties involved have been overcome in a number of cases[*] with the following results. Only a few cases can be taken up here: Dry hydrochloric acid gas does not decompose carbonates to any appreciable extent, and it does not precipitate silver nitrate dissolved in anydrous benzene or anhydrous ether. It does not change blue litmus red, nor does perfectly anhydrous sulphuric acid.

Dry hydrochloric acid gas does not react to any extent upon dry ammonia gas. In such an experiment it is, of course, necessary to take the greatest precautions in drying the gases, by allowing them to come in contact with the most powerful drying agents, under the most favorable

conditions, for a long period of time. This is a very surprising fact, but is even surpassed by the fo lowing experiment. Dry sodium can be dipped into sulphuric acid, from which every trace of moisture has been removed, without any appreciable action taking place. In this experiment, also, the greatest precautions must, of course, be taken to remove every trace of moisture from the substances, and from the vessels in which the experiments are to be carried out.

These experiments would show that molecules such as we have been considering do not have the power to react chemically; but these experiments alone do not justify the conclusion that other molecules may not react chemically, or that molecules under other conditions may not react. Any conclusion on this point could be drawn only after an elaborate study of chemical reactions in general, under very widely different conditions.

The result of such a study has, however, made it very probable that *molecules cannot react chemically with molecules.* It is possible that molecules may react with ions, but this is not proved.

It is very easy for any one whose knowledge of the facts is not very comprehensive, to think they have found examples of chemical activity where there are no ions present; but it should be remembered that not only water but most other solvents have some ionizing power, although this differs greatly from solvent to solvent. Furthermore, heat has a very great power of breaking down molecules into ions; fused salts being very considerably dissociated.

THE TWO GREAT GENERALIZATIONS.

In the first chapter we traced the discovery of the generalization that the gas-laws apply to the osmotic pressures of solutions; in the second and third, the origin of the theory of electrolytic dissociations and a few of its applications to chemical problems.

It is difficult to overestimate the importance of these generalizations for modern physical, and especially chemical science. Upon them has been built most of the science of modern physical chemistry, of which electrochemistry is only one chapter. It is not an exaggeration to say that every important development in electrochemistry, in the last dozen or fifteen years, has centred around one or the other of these generalizations, or around both.

The remaining chapters of this series of papers, will be devoted to a discussion of some of the more interesting and important advances, which have been made in electrochemistry since these generalizations were discovered.

CHAPTER IV—ELECTROLYSIS AND THEORIES OF ELECTROLYSIS.

PART I.

THERE are few subjects in electro-chemistry which have attracted more attention than the power of the current to decompose chemical compounds. This action has been known almost as long as the current itself. It was impossible to study these phenomena when the only source of electricity was that produced by friction, since a continuous supply could not be obtained for any appreciable length of time. Almost as soon as Volta discovered the pile which bears his name, these phenomena began to attract attention; but the first who made an extensive study of the power of the current to decompose chemical compounds was Sir Humphrey Davy. As is well known, he constructed the most powerful electrical battery which had been devised up to that time, and with this he was able to effect decompositions which had never been suspected as possible. His classical experiments, in which he decomposed potassium and sodium hydroxides, and discovered the alkali metals, are so well known that they need only a brief reference in this connection. Portions of his battery, and his notebooks in which these and other important discoveries are recorded, are still preserved at the Royal Institution, London, in connection with which much of his work was done.

THE WORK OF FARADAY.

There is, however, still one greater name in connection with the subject of electrolysis, and that is Faraday. For a considerable time Davy's assist-ant, and later his successor at the Royal Institution, Faraday continued the work which Davy had begun, and made discoveries of incomparably greater value. While Davy's work was mainly qualitative, testing what decompositions the current could effect, the work of Faraday was quantitative. He wished to know how much of given substances are decomposed by given amounts of the current, and whether the amount of decomposition was always proportional to the amount of current used, regardless of the source of the current. He tested the latter point in this manner: Currents of electricity produced in different ways were passed through solutions of the same substance, and the amount of decomposition determined. He found that a given amount of current always produces the same amount of decomposition, no matter what the source of the current may be. He then used different amounts of current, and studied the amounts of decomposition effected. *The amount of decomposition was always proportional to the amount of current used.* This may be termed the first law of Faraday.

Faraday went much farther and studied the decomposition of different substances by the same current, to see if any simple relations existed between the amounts of the different substances decomposed. He accomplished this by passing the same current through solutions of salts of a number of the metals, and determined the amounts of metals which were deposited. The result was the discovery of his well-known second law, that *the amounts of the different metals deposited by the same current are proportional to the chemical equivalents of these metals.* If we are dealing with the salts of univalent metals, the amounts deposited are proportional to the atomic weights of these elements; if we are dealing with bivalent elements the amounts deposited are proportional to the atomic weights of the elements divided by two; if with trivalent elements, to the atomic weights divided by three; if with *n*-valent elements, to the atomic weights divided by *n*.

These two laws are the most important discoveries which have ever been made in connection with electrolysis, and both of them we owe to Faraday, who also gave us the *Electrochemical Nomenclature,* which we use up to the present time. He termed the parts in solution which move as the current is passed, *ions;* those which move in the solution with the current, *cations,* and those which move opposite to the current, *anions.* The substance which, in solution, undergoes decomposition by the current he called an electrolyte, and the process by which these substances are decomposed *electrolysis.* The places at which the decomposition manifested itself he termed the *poles* or *electrodes;* that pole toward which the cations move he called the *cathode,* that towards which the anions move, the *anode.*

Faraday distinguished sharply between two classes of conductors: Those which carry the current without undergoing decomposition, such as the metals, carbon, etc., which he termed conductors of the *first class;* and those which undergo decomposition at the electrodes, such as solutions of acids, bases, and salts, which he termed conductors of the second class.

That there is a sharp distinction between the two classes of conductors, seems to be doubtful at present. Recent work has made it probable that the metals conduct by means of ions, as solutions of electrolytes conduct by means of ions; the difference in the results obtained being, in part, due to the different conditions which surround the ions in the metal and in the solution.

TESTING THE LAW OF FARADAY.

There are few laws in nature which have been subjected to more rigid experimental test than the law of Faraday. Conditions have been varied wherever it was possible, to see whether the law would hold. It appeared a few years ago as if exceptions had been discovered to the law. If a current is passed through solutions of certain electrolytes, which are subjected to a high pressure, there is slightly less decomposition effected by a given quantity of current than if the solution of the electrolyte is under normal pressure. This was not explained for a time, other than as an exception to the law of Faraday. A perfectly satisfactory explanation has, however, been furnished. When the liquid is subjected to high pressure, more of the air above it is forced into solution, and a small part of the oxygen, or nitrogen, or both, is ionized by the solvent. These ions help to carry the current from one electrode to the other, with the result that more current passes than would correspond to the amount of metal separated upon the cathode.

The law of Faraday has, then, withstood all tests, and is one of the few laws of nature to which no exceptions are known.

ELECTROCHEMICAL THEORIES.

The discovery that chemical compounds can be decomposed by the current, seemed to make it probable that there was a very close connection between chemical attraction and electrical attraction. This idea was further strengthened by the fact that in the voltaic cell we have chemical action going on, and an electric current produced. Chemical action and electrical action thus seemed, in a sense, to be complementary. When an electric current was passed through a solution containing certain chemical compounds, these compounds were broken down; the chemical attraction which held them together being overcome. Conversely, in the cell we have chemical compounds being formed, and at the same time a current was generated.

These relations were thought by Davy to be very close, as we shall see from the theory which he proposed to account for chemical union. According to the *Electrochemical Theory of Davy* the atoms of different substances exist in an uncharged condition; but when they come in contact they become charged—the one positively and the other negatively. These positively and negatively charged atoms attract one another, just as any other positively and negatively charged bodies would do; the force of the attraction for a given distance depending upon the magnitude of the difference between the charges. The electrolysis of a compound, in terms of the electrochemical theory of Davy, consists in the separation at the poles of the different elements in an uncharged condition. The negatively charged atom is attracted to the positive pole, and, having its potential raised to zero by addition of positive electricity, separates on this pole

in a neutral condition. Similarly, the positively charged particle is attracted to the negative pole, and, through addition of negative electricity becomes electrically neutral and separates from the solution in this condition.

The electrochemical theory of Davy never came into prominence, and never seems to have exerted any marked influence on chemical thought. Shortly after it was proposed it was entirely overshadowed by another electrochemical theory; *viz.*, that of Berzelius.

THE ELECTROCHEMICAL THEORY OF BERZELIUS.

The electrochemical theory of Berzelius differs fundamentally from that of Davy, in that it assumes that the *atoms are charged before they come in contact.* The natural condition of the atom is to be charged, and, indeed, both positively and negatively. These opposite charges exist upon the atom in polar arrangement, but either the positive or negative charge predominates in magnitude, so that the algebraic sum of the charges upon any atom is always either a positive or a negative quantity, and never zero. Every atom acts, then, as if it were charged either positively or negatively.

Chemical attraction is nothing but the electrical attraction of these oppositely charged atoms; the magnitude of the attraction depending upon the difference between the charges upon the atoms which enter into the compound. When the differently charged atoms come in contact the electrical differences would disappear, and then the atoms would fall asunder, since the attraction which held them together no longer exists. This seems to be a weak point in the electrochemical theory of Berzelius. However, as quickly as the atoms part company, the electrical differences would be reestablished, and they would again attract one another, and we would have a continual decomposition and recombination taking place.

Another objection was urged against the electrochemical theory of Berzelius, which led to its abandonment for more than half a century. If chemical attraction is nothing but the electrical attraction of oppositely charged parts, then the properties of the compound formed must be a function of the electrical charges upon the atoms. If any two compounds resembled one another closely in properties, the electrical charges upon the atoms must be closely analogous. It was found that the two compounds, acetic acid and trichloracetic acid, are closely allied in their chemical and physical properties. In the latter we have three atoms of chlorine corresponding to three atoms of hydrogen in the former, as can be seen at once by comparing their formulas:

Acetic Acid.   Trichloracetic Acid.
CH_3COOH. CCl_3COOH.

It was reasoned that the hydrogen atoms in acetic acid, like the hydrogen atoms under all other conditions, are charged positively; and the chlorine atoms which have replaced them, like all other chlorine atoms, are charged negatively. We have thus, replaced three positive charges in acetic acid by three negative charges, and have not materially changed the nature of the compound. This argument was too much for Berzelius, and in spite of many attempts was never answered satisfactorily by him. The result was that his theory fell into disrepute, and was simply regarded as a convenient means of classifying substances,

without in any wise being a correct expression of the facts.

THOMSON OVERTHROWS THE OBJECTIONS
TO THE ELECTROCHEMICAL THEORY
OF BERZELIUS.

This objection to the Berzelius theory, which passed muster for considerably more than half a century, has recently been entirely overthrown by the work of J. J. Thomson.* He took a glass tube, closed at both ends, and sealed platinum electrodes into the two ends. A sheet of aluminum was placed across the middle of the tube, but did not fit tightly against the glass walls; the tube was filled with vapors of chloroform, which is methane in which three of the hydrogen atoms have been replaced by chlorine. This will be seen from the formulas of the two substances:

Methane.   Chloroform.
CH_4. CCl_3H.

If marsh gas is electrolyzed by passing the current between the electrodes, the hydrogen, like other positively charged substances, would move toward the *negative* pole. We would suppose that the chlorine in chloroform, being negatively charged, would pass to the positive pole; but Thomson found that *it also went to the negative pole.* This showed that *the chlorine in chloroform was not negatively charged, as had been supposed, but was positively charged.*

The importance of this discovery cannot easily be overestimated. It shows, conclusively, that the same atom may, under different conditions, have entirely different charges upon it, since we know that chlorine is usually negative. It

* For a detailed account of Thomson's experiment, see *Nature*, 51, 455. Also Theory of Electrolytic Dissociation, Jones, p. 41.

shows, further, that *atoms of positive hydrogen are replaced by atoms of positive chlorine.* This throws entirely new light on the whole nature of substitution in chemistry, making it probable that atoms carrying one kind of electricity are only replaced by atoms carrying a charge of the same nature; *i.e.,* positive atoms by positive, and negative atoms by negative.

The bearing upon the argument against the electrochemical theory of Berzelius is at once obvious. The *three positive hydrogen atoms* in acetic acid are replaced by *three positive chlorine atoms,* and the nature of the two compounds should from the theory, as they are in fact, be very closely allied.

We recognize to-day that the electrochemical theory of Berzelius contains a large element of truth, and is one of the forerunners of the theory of electrolytic dissociation.

OLDER THEORIES TO ACCOUNT FOR ELECTROLYSIS.

Almost as quickly as the facts connected with electrolysis became known, attempts were made to account for these facts in terms of conceptions which then prevailed. This is the usual course of procedure. The thinking mind is never content with the discovery of isolated facts, nor even of facts which bear some vague relations to one another. It wants to know what deep-seated relation really exists between the facts; it desires to correlate the facts and see if possible what they really mean. "The aim of research, says a distinguished man of science, is not the discovery of facts, but the discovery of generalizations, and the more one thinks over this proposition the more one sees the deep meaning which it

contains. Facts, and theory or generalization, bear about the same relation to each other as the bricks and a magnificent piece of architecture. The bricks are absolutely essential to the structure, but they, in themselves, are not the aim of the architect. The aim of science is to discover these great truths of nature which we call generalizations, and the facts are the essentials out of which the edifice of truth is built.

The first to propose *a Theory of Electrolysis was Grotthuss,* in 1805. This theory is now only of interest historically, yet, for the sake of the development of our subject, it must be considered. The facts which had to be accounted for at that time were comparatively few. It was known that when a little acid is added to water to make it conducting, as they said, and a current is passed, hydrogen was liberated at the cathode and oxygen at the anode. This was explained by Grotthuss as follows: Let us think of a layer of water molecules between the anode and the cathode. Starting at the cathode we would have a hydrogen atom with a positive charge. This would give up its positive charge to the pole and escape as hydrogen gas. The oxygen atom, which was originally combined with this hydrogen, is now free and combines with the hydrogen atom of the next molecule of water. This sets free another oxygen atom, which combines with the next hydrogen, and so on until the anode is reached, when the last free oxygen atom gives up its charge to this pole and escape as oxygen gas.

The feature of this theory which distinguishes it from subsequent theories is that in water every hydrogen atom is

* See Theory of Electrolytic Dissociation.

firmly and fixedly combined with a definite oxygen atom, and never parts company with it until the current is passed.

The above theory accounted for all the facts which were known at the time it was proposed, but it was soon discovered that a current which is far too weak to decompose a molecule of water would still effect the electrolysis of acidified water. This could not be accounted for at all by the theory of Grotthuss, and led to a *new electrochemical theory, that of Clausius*. The theory of Clausius, which was proposed in 1856, has already been referred to in connection with the development of the theory of electrolytic dissociation. The distinctive feature of the theory of Clausius, as we have seen, is that it assumes that before the current is passed a small number of water molecules are already broken down into parts or ions. This would account for the fact just referred to, that an infinitesimal current, which is far too weak to decompose a molecule of water, can effect the electrolysis of water. The action of such a current is simply a directing one, driving the anions toward the anode and the cations toward the cathode, where they lose their charges and separate in the uncharged condition. We have already seen that the theory of Clausius is the immediate forerunner of the theory of electrolytic dissociation, and we shall see a little later in this paper, is connected quite closely with the theory of electrolysis which we hold to-day. We shall now take up the newer theories of electrolysis.

CHAPTER IV–ELECTROLYSIS AND THEORIES ELECTROLYSIS.

PART II.

THE NEWER THEORIES OF ELECTROLYSIS.

The theory of electrolysis which was held until a few years ago, had to take into account the following facts: When a current is passed through a solution of an acid, hydrogen separates at the cathode and oxygen at the anode. This was true, in general, but there were some exceptions as in the case of the electrolysis of a hot, concentrated, solution of hydrochloric acid, where chlorine separated at the anode. If the solution of the acid was dilute the above statement may be taken as general.

If a dilute solution of a base is electrolyzed, hydrogen separates upon the cathode and oxygen upon the anode, in the same way as if an acid was used.

If a dilute solution of a salt is electrolyzed, we will have different results, depending upon the nature of the salt which is used. If we select a salt of a metal which decomposes water, say of the alkalies or alkaline earths, we will have, on electrolysis, oxygen liberated at the anode and hydrogen liberated at the cathode. If, on the other hand, we electrolyze a salt of a metal which does not decompose water, as for example copper, we would have oxygen set free at the anode, and instead of hydrogen being liberated at the cathode, we would have metallic copper deposited upon this pole.

Take first the case of an acid; say hydrochloric acid. The hydrogen ions move with the current over to the cathode, give up their charge to it and escape as hydro-gen gas. The chlorine ions move ag[?] the current over to the anode, give[?] their negative charge, but do not es[?] as chlorine unless the solution is hot concentrated. The chlorine acts upon water in the sense of the following e[?] tion,.

$$H_2O + 2Cl = 2HCl + O,$$

forming hydrochloric acid and setting gen free. Two atoms of oxygen com[?] forming a molecule, which then escap[?] ordinary gaseous oxygen; the hydroch[?] acid remaining in the solution again dergoes electrolysis as described above, the process is continuous. Take the of a base; say potassium hydroxide. hydroxyl ions move against the cu[?] over to the anode, give up their neg[?] charges to it, and cannot escape as ox[?] and hydrogen, but two hydroxyl gr[?] react forming a molecule of water and oxygen, thus:

$$2(OH) = H_2O + O.$$

The potassium cation moves with the rent over to the cathode, gives u[?] charge and becomes a potassium ato[?] potassium atom cannot, of course, e[?] the presence of water without acting [?] ically upon it, in the sense of the f[?] ing equation:

$$K + H_2O = KOH + H$$

forming potassium hydroxide and ting hydrogen free. Two atoms of hy[?] gen then combine, forming a mole[?] which escapes as ordinary hydrogen The potassium hydroxide formed u[?]

goes electrolysis as above described, and this process, like that where an acid was employed, is a continuous one.

Take, finally, the electrolysis of a salt. Here we have two cases to deal with, as has already been stated. Take first the simpler case, where the metal in the salt does not decompose water—say copper sulphate. The copper cation moves to the cathode, gives up its charge and separates as metallic copper. The SO_4 anion moves to the anode, gives up its charge, but cannot escape. It acts upon a molecule of water, thus,

$$H_2O + SO_4 = H_2SO_4 + O,$$

forming oxygen which escapes, and generating sulphuric acid, which remains in the solution as such if platinum electrodes are employed, or acts upon the electrodes if copper or a similar metal is used; forming the sulphate again which then undergoes electrolysis, as above described. If copper electrodes are used, this process also is continuous.

Let us now take the salt of a metal which decomposes water—say potassium sulphate. The anion $\overline{SO}_4$ passes to the anode, and the process at this electrode is exactly as just described, but a very different condition obtains at the cathode. The ion potassium moves to the cathode, gives up its charge and becomes an atom. This reacts with water, as in the case where a base was electrolyzed, forming potassium hydroxide and setting hydrogen free. The potassium hydroxide formed at the cathode reacts chemically with the sulphuric acid formed at the anode, and gives potassium sulphate, which then undergoes electrolysis again as just described. This would continue until all the water present had been decomposed.

The essential feature of this theory is

that water is decomposed by the products of electrolysis, either at the anode as in the case of an acid; or at the cathode in the case of a base; or at the anode in the case of a salt whose metal does not decompose water; or at both the anode and cathode in the case of a salt whose metal does decompose water. The leading feature to bear in mind is that the *water is not decomposed by the current directly, but that the decomposition of water is a secondary process,* being effected by the primary products of electrolysis, which separate at the poles and then act chemically upon the water present, liberating either oxygen or hydrogen gas.

THIS THEORY NOT SUFFICIENT TO-DAY.

The theory which has just been discussed seems to account so satisfactorily for all the facts, that we would naturally ask, why look farther for a new or different theory? The above theory was sufficient for nearly a half-century, but facts have been discovered in the last few years which show that it is no longer tenable.

In the first place it has been shown that although hydrogen and hydroxyl ions cannot exist in the presence of each other uncombined to any large extent, yet *water is always slightly dissociated.* The best results seem to indicate that about one molecule of water in every million exists in the form of ions. The discovery of this fact very appreciably complicates the whole problem of electrolysis, since we have to take into account not only the cations and anions which come from the electrolyte, but also those which come from the dissociated water which is always present. Take the case of a very simple salt like sodium chloride. Around the cathode we not only have sodium cations, but also hydrogen cations; and around the anode not only chlorine anions, but hydroxyl anions. The question is, then, when the current is passed which cations and which anions will give up their charges? It is obvious that that kind of cations and anions which hold their charges *less firmly* will give them up. According to the theory which we have just considered, these are the sodium cations and the chlorine anions. But this theory would also have these ions, which hold their charges less firmly than the hydrogen and hydroxyl ions, and therefore give them up, take the charges from the hydrogen and hydroxyl ions, respectively, becoming sodium and chlorine ions again. This theory, therefore, contains, in the light of recent experimental discoveries, a self-evident contradiction, and can no longer be regarded as satisfactory.

THE PRESENT THEORY OF ELECTROLYSIS.

It is a very much simpler matter to show that a prevailing conception is not tenable, than to propose a theory which will accord with all the facts known, and predict relations as yet undiscovered. It is obvious from the above, that we must abandon the theory of electrolysis which involves the secondary decomposition of water, and look about for a more satisfactory explanation. We shall take up first the theory of electrolysis which is held to-day, and then look to the experimental evidence upon which it is based.

When a current is passed through a solution of hydrochloric acid, we have the hydrogen ions moving toward the cathode, and chlorine ions toward the anode. These are experimental facts, which are independent of any theory. We have, then, around the cathode, hydrogen ions from the dissociated acid, and also hydrogen ions from the dissociated water. Since, however, any hydrogen ion is just like any other hydrogen ion, it does not matter which we regard as giving up its charge to the cathode and escaping as gaseous hydrogen. Around the anode, however, we have two different kinds of anions—chlorine from the dissociated acid and hydroxyl from the dissociated water. Which will give up its charge to the pole? Obviously, the one which holds it less firmly. According to the old theory it is the chlorine, but according to the new it is the hydroxyl. Two hydroxyl anions lose their negative charges and then form a molecule of water, setting oxygen free which escapes from the solution. The chlorine anions[1] suffer no change at the pole; they simply serve to carry the negative current to this electrode, and reform hydrochloric acid with the hydrogen ions of the water.

If we are electrolyzing potassium hydroxide, the facts are that potassium ions move toward the cathode, while hydroxyl ions move toward the anode. Around the cathode we have, then, two kinds of cations —potassium, coming from the hydroxide and hydrogen, coming from the dissociated portion of the water. Around the anode, however, we have only one kind of anions —hydroxyl coming from the dissociated base, and hydroxyl coming from the dissociated water. The case is the reverse of that which exists when an acid was employed. In the latter case there was a common cation, hydrogen; in the case of a base a common anion, hydroxyl.

When a current is passed through a solution of a base the hydroxyl anions give up their charges to the anode, and

---

[1] Hydrochloric acid was selected to illustrate the theory, for the sake of simplicity. As a matter of fact chlorine ions give up their charges more readily than hydroxyl, but this does not interfere with the use of this simple substance as an illustration.

form water and oxygen. At the cathode the old theory said it was the potassium ions which gave up their charges, while the new says it is the hydrogen ions from the dissociated water. The potassium cations serve. to carry the positive current to the cathode, and form again at this electrode potassium hydroxide with the hydroxyl ions of the water.

The electrolysis of a salt is a little more complicated, but presents no serious difficulty. Take sodium chloride, whose ions are sodium which move to the cathode, and chlorine which move to the anode. We have two kinds of cations around the cathode, sodium and hydrogen; and two kinds of anions around the anode, chlorine and hydroxyl. At the cathode the hydrogen ions give up their charges and escape as gaseous hydrogen; the potassium cations forming potassium hydroxide with the hydroxyl ions from the water. At the anode the hydroxyl anions give up their charges, forming water, and oxygen which escapes; the chlorine anions forming hydrochloric acid with the hydrogen ions from the dissociated water. The base formed at the cathode can then react with the acid formed at the anode and regenerate the salt.

It will be observed that this theory differs fundamentally from the one which was held for such a long time, in that it represents the decomposition of water as being effected directly by the current. We have here *the primary decomposition of water* in electrolysis, while the older theory represented the decomposition of water as a secondary process, produced by the products of electrolysis acting chemically upon the water.

It should be observed that this theory of electrolysis resembles in a striking man-

ner the very early theories, in that it represents the water as being decomposed directly by the current—the electrolyte simply serving to carry the current through the solution, or, as it was said, to make the water a conductor. The new theory, of course, incorporates much that was not contained in the old, having the advantage of a half-century of investigation on these and similar problems.

It is, as we have said, not such a difficult matter to propose a theory as it is to test its truth. How can the theory which we have just considered be tested experimentally?

TESTING THE PRESENT THEORY OF ELEC-
TROLYSIS.

The theory with which we are now dealing could be readily tested experimentally, if we had some means of determining in any given case which of two ions would give up their charge most readily. Such a means has been furnished by Le Blanc, to whom we owe the whole theory which we have just described.

If we attempt to pass a current through a solution of any electrolyte, the result will be dependent upon the electromotive force of the current. If this is below a certain value the current will flow for an instant and then cease to flow, as can be shown by interposing a galvanometer in the circuit of the current. When the current has reached a certain electromotive force, which varies for different electrolytes employed, it will flow continuously, and electrolysis will take place, as already described. This minimum electromotive force, which will just drive the current continuously through the solution of the electrolyte, is known as the "Polarization Minimum," or "Decomposition Value" of the substance in question. It means that this electromotive force, or potential, is required to cause the particular ions with which we are dealing to give up their charges. By studying the decomposition values of different electrolytes, including acids, bases, and salts, we obtain exactly the data which we need to test this theory —we learn the relative ease with which the different ions give up their charges. A few of the decomposition values of the more common acids, bases, and salts, in normal solution, are given below:

	Decomposition Value.
Sulphuric acid	1.67 vol s.
Nitric "	1.69 "
Phosphoric "	1.70 "
Monochloracetic a id	1.72 "
Dichloracetic "	1 66 "
Malonic "	1 69 "
Sodium hydroxide	1 69 "
Potassium "	1.67 "
Ammonium "	1.74 "
Barium nitrate	2.25 "
Stron ium "	2.28 "
Calcium "	2 11 "
Potassium "	2.17 "
Sodium "	2.15 "

These are the facts. Let us now see what bearing they have upon the theory in hand. According to this theory the electrolysis of any one *salt* is the same process as the electrolysis of any other salt, since the ions from the salt simply carry the current; while it is the hydrogen and hydroxyl ions from the dissociated water which give up their charges to, and separate at the poles. The decomposition values of salts are the decomposition values of hydrogen and hydroxyl ions, at the concentrations which obtain, and should be practically the same for all salts. The above results for the decomposition values of salts show that fact and theory are in satisfactory accord.

Take the case of *acids*. These dissociate into hydrogen cations, and into anions whose nature depends upon the acid used. Take nitric acid; the gen cations move to the cathode, gi their charges and escape, as we seen. The anions move to the but do not give up their charges hydroxyl anions from the water gi their charges instead; an equal num hydrogen ions from the dissociated remaining in solution and refo nitric acid with the anions. must, therefore, be a constant deco tion value for acids, which correspo the potential required to discharg droxyl ions on the one hand, and hyd ions on the other, under the conditi concentrations which obtain. Such i from the decomposition values of given above, to be the case. This sponds to about 1.7 volts for normal tions of acids.

The facts and theory agree so wel acids, we should naturally turn n *bases.* These yield hydroxyl ions give up their charges to the anode, water, and oxygen which escapes. cations move to the cathode, but give up their charges; the hydrogen from the water giving up their ch instead. We have here exactly the processes taking place as in the el ysis of acids, and the decomposition of bases should be the same as th acids of the same concentration, sinc are the decomposition values of hy and hydroxyl ions, the product of concentration is a constant. Fact theory, therefore, agree as well in th of bases as of acids and salts.

There is, however, still one more which must be considered in conn with the decomposition values given in order that the line of reasoning these values may be complete.

"Acids* and bases of the same concentration must have the same decomposition values, as we have seen, because the product of the number of hydrogen and hydroxyl ions in such solutions must, from the law of mass action, always remain constant. It is, however, quite different with a salt. At the cathode hydrogen is liberated and a base is formed, which means an increase in the number of hydroxyl ions around this pole; and, similarly, the formation of an acid around the anode increases the number of hydrogen ions around the anode. Since the product of the number of hydrogen and hydroxyl ions which can remain in a solution is a constant, an increase in the number of hydroxyl ions means a decrease in the number of the hydrogen ions present around the cathode; and, similarly, an increase in the number of hydrogen ions around the anode would diminish the number of hydroxyl ions around this pole. Both of these influences would increase the decomposition value.

Here, again, theory and fact are in perfect accord. A comparison of the decomposition values of acids and bases, with those of salts, will show that the latter are considerably larger than the maximum values for the former.

The evidence for the present theory of electrolysis is, then, so satisfactory that we cannot hesitate in accepting it as a highly probable explanation of what takes place when a current is passed through a solution of an acid, base, or salt.

The great difficulty which has been encountered in dealing with a process, apparently no more complicated than the electrolysis of an acid, should be noted.

It is a general fact that Nature deals out her truth with a sparing hand, and only as the reward of an enormous amount of labor.

THE ELECTROLYTIC SEPARATION OF THE METALS.

There are one or two other matters which must be considered before this chapter is closed, since they are of the very deepest significance for the practical electrochemist. It is not only possible to deposit many of the metals from their ores by means of the current, but to separate the metals from one another electrolytically. In obtaining the metals from their ores, or in purifying them after they have been obtained in a crude form, the conditions under which the electrolysis is effected are somewhat modified from case to case. The great problem here is to use electrodes which are not attacked by the products of electrolysis, and to so modify the conditions that "the yield" may be made as large as possible. For details in this connection reference only can be made to some comprehensive work.* Suffice it to say that sodium, potassium, lithium, barium, calcium, strontium, aluminium, copper, silver, gold, platinum, and many other metals are now readily obtained by electrolysis.

The problem of electrolytic separation of the metals is of special interest in connection with the matters which we have just considered. If a current is passed through a solution containing several kinds of ions, all of these will take part in carrying the current; the amount carried by any one kind of ions depending upon the relative number of these which are present, and upon their velocity. When these reach the electrode, those with

---

*From "Elements of Physical Chemistry," by H C. Jones, which will be published in the near future by the Macmillans.

*Borchers' "Elektrometallurgie."

the lowest decomposition values will separate first. If the difference in potential between the electrolyte and electrode is less than the decomposition value of any ion, this will not give up its charge.

The decomposition values of the different ions are very different, and this makes it possible to effect electrolytic separations of the metals. A current of electromotive force just small enough to cause the ion with the lowest decomposition value to separate, is used at first. The electromotive force of the current is then increased until the decomposition value of the next ion is reached, when it will separate, and so on. After all the ions of any given element have separated, the current will cease to flow until its electromotive force has been raised to the decomposition value of the ion next in the series, so that it is not very difficult in practice to so regulate the conditions that good quantitative separations can be effected.

It has, however, been clearly recognized that current strength or current density is an important factor in electrolytic separations, since it conditions the number of ions which will separate in any given time. If the density is great, the ions are rushed over to the electrode so rapidly that time is not given for all the more easily discharged ions to reach the electrode by diffusion, etc., and some of the ions with higher decomposition values may separate. The result is that under these conditions only partial separations are secured.

From the study of the decomposition values of the ions by Le Blanc, Freudenberg, and others in Ostwald's laboratory, the whole subject of the electrolytic separations of the metals was opened up

The electrolytic action of the current has also been applied to organic compounds, with some remarkable results. Organic acids, as has been stated, dissociate into a hydrogen cation and an anion which comprises the remainder of the molecule. As is well known, organic anions are always complex, and in many cases are very complicated groups. These groups, when they separate at the anode, are generally incapable of existence as such, and either combine with one another and form new products, or break down into simpler substances. Thus, the anion of acetic acid, CH_3COO holds its charge less firmly than hydroxyl, and when it arrives at the anode it gives up its charge, and then, being incapable of existence as such, breaks down in the sense of the following equation:

$$2CH_3CO_2 = C_2H_6 + 2CO_2.$$

The anion of propionic acid breaks down as follows

$$2C_2H_5CO_2 = C_2H_5COOH + C_2H_4.$$

The electrolysis of organic bases has yielded similar results in the few cases which have been studied. The cation of the organic base is too complex to exist uncharged, and when it gives up its charge, reactions take place giving rise to new products. The electrolysis of organic acids has already become an important means of effecting the synthesis of organic compounds, and an examination of the literature will show that the result already obtained are not only of scientific value, but have found their way into the factories as means of synthesizing organic dyestuffs and the like.

The electrolysis of organic compounds is not limited to the acids and bases, but has been extended to other classes of substances, such as the esters. Thus, when the monoethyl ester of malonic acid, rather, the potassium salt of this ester, is subjected to electrolysis, the following reaction takes place:

$$2CH_2\begin{array}{l}COOK\\COOC_2H_5\end{array}=\begin{array}{l}CH_2COOC_2H_5\\CH_2COOC_2H_5\end{array}\\+2CO_2+2K.$$

From the monoester of a dibasic acid, the diester of a dibasic acid richer in carbon was thus obtained. Walker found that this was a more or less general method for passing from one dibasic acid to another richer in carbon atoms.

The application of electrolysis to organic compounds has been just fairly begun, and from what has already been accomplished, it seems probable that much of interest to the man of science and also to the practical electrician, will be discovered in this field.

We have here, then, both in inorganic chemistry and in organic, important branches of industry developed directly out of investigations undertaken and carried out in the interest of pure science. Indeed, this is almost invariably the order of progress. The investigator works and discovers the truth purely for its own sake, just because he desires to know what it is. The practical man applies the knowledge thus obtained to the welfare of the human race, often, however, adding greatly to it. The importance not only of accurate scientific knowledge, but of scientific investigation in the factory and in the shop, is being felt to such an extent that it has become an absolute necessity; and we see to-day in the large German, and other factories, investigation being carried on to an enormous extent. There is one chemical factory in Germany where more than 100 trained chemists are employed to carry out investigations alone, and many others with a smaller number; and this suggests another thought. The men selected to carry out investigations in the great factories and shops in the world are not men who have had a narrow, one-sided, training, in a few things, but those who have had broad training along purely scientific lines. It is now fully recognized that men who have been trained first in pure science are best equipped for any line of technical work. In a word, the proper place to lay the foundation for the career of the practical man is in the University.

The next chapter will deal with the velocities with which the ions move through solutions, and some of the methods for determining these velocities.

CHAPTER V—ON THE VELOCITY OF IONS.

WE HAVE referred repeatedly in our last chapter to the movements of the ions during electrolysis; the cations moving with the current toward the cathode, the anions against the current toward the anode. Since, from the law of Faraday, electricity can pass through solutions of electrolytes in only one way, by the simultaneous movement toward, and separation of the ions at the electrodes, it is obvious that the study of the velocities with which the ions travel under given conditions, is a matter of considerable importance.

There are really two problems involved in determining the velocities of the ions: First, the determination of the relative velocities with which the ions move; and, second, the determination of the absolute velocities with which the ions move. If the relative velocities of all the ions have once been determined, and the absolute velocity of any one ion is known, the absolute velocities of all the ions can be calculated at once. We shall take up first the determination of the relative velocities of ions.

It is not a simple matter to see at once how the ions can move with very different velocities toward the poles, and yet the same number or same equivalence of ions separate at the two poles. No cation can separate at the cathode until an anion separates at the anode, and for every ion which separates at one pole an ion carrying the opposite charge must separate at the other pole. It may, of course, happen that one of the ions is bivalent and the other univalent. In this case, for every

bivalent ion which separates at one two univalent ions will separate other. This is obvious from Far law, which refers the whole concept chemical valence to the number of cl carried by the ions.

In consideration of the confusion usually arises from the contemplati the above problem for the first time with a desire to simplify it, Ostwal posed the following illustration of takes place when a current is through a solution of an electrolyte, cations and anions move with dif velocities. Given a homogeneous sol which always contains the same num cations and anions, and let us say th velocity of the anion is *twice* as gr that of the cation. Let us represer anions thus, ○, and let us represer cations thus, ⊖. In such a solutio would have the following arrangeme the parts:

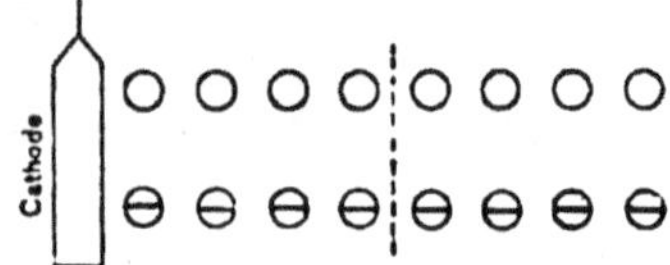

Fig. 2.—Ions in a Homogeneous Solu

For every anion there would be sponding cation, and before the cu was passed there would, of course, decomposition of the electrolyte. perpendicular dotted line does not a partition running down through solution, but is simply to indicat middle of the solution.

Let a current be now passed th

the solution, the anode and cathode being placed in the positions indicated in the above sketch. We can allow the current to pass until any number of molecules are decomposed; but for the sake of simplicity let the current flow until *three* molecules have been electrolyzed, and their ions caused to separate at the two poles. The following condition would then obtain in the solution:

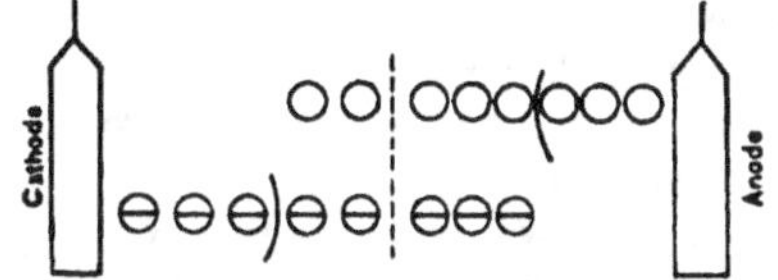

Fig. 3.—Solution after Three Molecules are Electrolyzed.

We would have three anions separated at the anode, as shown by the three circles unpaired with cations; and we should, of course, have three cations separated at the cathode, as is shown by three lined circles unpaired with anions. The important part of the problem, however, from the standpoint of relative velocities of ions, still remains to be considered. Let us discard the anions and cations which have

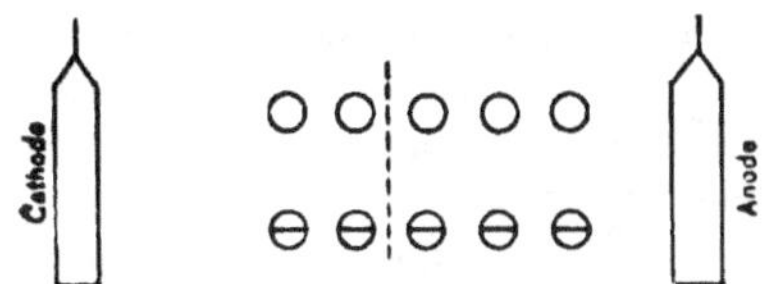

Fig. 4.—Condition of Remaining Solution.

given up their charges, respectively, to the anode and cathode, and consider the condition of the solution which remains. It would be as shown in Fig. 4.

The same number of anions and cations are, of course, present in the solution, but their positions relative to the central plane running through the solution, are very different from the positions occupied before the current was passed. In the

original solution we had four anions and four cations on each side of the central plane. We have now only three anions and three cations on the right side of this plane, and only two anions and two cations on the left side of the plane. The conditions are thus markedly different; the original solution having lost one anion and one cation on the right side next to the anode, and two anions and two cations on the left side next to the cathode.

This illustration not only serves to show how the same number of anions and cations separate at the two poles, and yet the velocities of the two kinds of ions be very different, but also gives us the clue to the principle involved in determining the relative velocities of ions. It has been observed that on the anode side of the solution there is a loss of *one* molecule, and on the cathode side of the solution there is a loss of *two* molecules, the total number of molecules decomposed being *three*. The above numbers, one and two, bear exactly the same relation to one another as the velocities with which, by hypothesis, the cations and anions travel. We thus arrive at the general rule: To determine the relative velocity of the anion, divide the change in concentration around the cathode by the total number of molecules decomposed. To determine the relative velocity of the cation divide the change in concentration around the anode by the total number of molecules decomposed.

So much by way of illustration of the principles involved. The more important question is how can these relative velocities be determined experimentally?

EXPERIMENTAL DETERMINATION OF THE RELATIVE VELOCITIES OF IONS.

It is obvious from what has been

said, that in order to determine the relative velocities of any given cation and anion, it is necessary to electrolyze a solution containing this cation and anion, and then to determine the changes in concentration around the electrodes. The current should be passed until an appreciable change in concentration has been produced, but must be discontinued while there is still a middle layer of the solution unacted upon. We must know, in addition to the changes in concentration around the poles, the total amount of the electrolyte decomposed. This can be measured either directly, or, more conveniently, by simply measuring the amount of current which has passed through the electrolyte. If we know the amount of current which has passed, from Faraday's law we can calculate at once the amount of the electrolyte decomposed. In practice the mode of procedure is as follows: The solution is placed in some convenient form of apparatus (which will be described a little later) and the current passed until a considerable change in concentration has been produced around the electrodes; the electrodes used being of the same metal as the cation of the solution.

The solution, whose concentration was originally known, is now analyzed around both electrodes, and the change in concentration produced by the current thus determined. The amount of current which has passed through the solution is then determined by some convenient method, usually by means of a silver voltameter inserted into the circuit; and we have all the data necessary for calculating the relative velocities of the two ions.

A large number of forms of apparatus have been employed, the object being to secure a simple and satisfactory separation of the solutions around the two electrodes, after the electrolysis has been ended. It is not unfair to say that many of the forms which have been devised and used, cannot be regarded as having accomplished this end in a satisfactory manner.

One of the most satisfactory forms, as it appears to me, taking all sides of the problem into account, was devised and used by W. T. Mather in the Johns Hopkins University.* This apparatus consists essentially of two upright tubes, which should be closed at the bottom by stopcocks. These are connected near the tops by a U tube, in the centre and at the lowest part of which a stop-cock of very large bore is inserted. The whole apparatus is thus perfectly symmetrical on the two sides. The electrodes were inserted into the bottom of the upright tubes, passing through ground-glass stoppers. It would be much better to have the bottoms of these tubes closed by stop-cocks, as stated above, and the electrodes pass into the tops of the tubes well down into the solutions on the two sides. The work in which this apparatus was used had to do with silver salts, consequently, silver electrodes were used.

The current, measured by means of a silver voltameter, was passed until the solutions in the two upright tubes around the electrodes had suffered considerable change in concentration. The current was interrupted while there was still an unaltered layer filling the U tube, the stopcock in this tube was closed, and then all the altered solution around each electrode was drawn off and analyzed. The change

* A brief account of this method has already appeared in the Johns Hopkins University circular. The full account of the work will soon appear in the *American Chemical Journal*.

in concentration around each electrode was thus determined.

The advantage of this apparatus over other forms, is that after the electrolysis

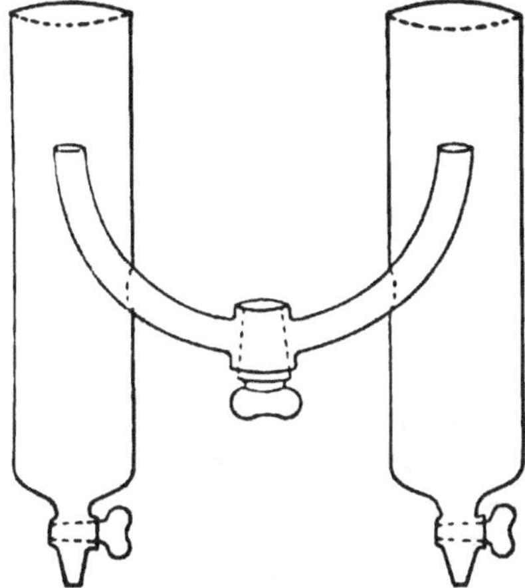

Fig. 5.—Apparatus for Measuring the Velocity of Ions.

is ended the two solutions can be readily separated and easily washed out of the vessel.

It is, in theory, not necessary to determine the changes in concentration around both electrodes, since the sum of these changes is always equal to the total amount of the electrolyte decomposed. It would be only necessary to determine the amount of current passed through the solution, which gives the total amount of the electrolyte decomposed, and the change in concentration around one electrode; the change in concentration around the other electrode being the difference between these two quantities.

In practice it is better to determine directly all the quantities, and use the sum of the two as a check on the value of the third.

INFLUENCES WHICH MAY AFFECT THE RELATIVE VELOCITIES OF IONS.

It does not follow that the relative velocity of ions obtained under one set of conditions will hold under different conditions. The relative velocity might change with the strength of current used, with the strength of the solution, or possibly temperature would have an influence which would be different with different ions. These points can be decided only by direct experiment.

Let us take up first the effect of *changing the strength of current* used in electrolyzing the solution. It is self-evident that the actual velocities with which the ions travel would be greatly affected by the strength of current employed; the greater the current, the greater the velocity of the ions required to carry the current. Since the actual velocities would be so greatly changed, it is not improbable that the influence on the different ions would be different; in a word, that the relative velocities would be changed.

Currents of very different strengths were used by Hittorf, who studied this problem experimentally. He found that for the strengths of current which he employed, the relative velocities are *independent* of the strength of the current.

It should be added that in all work on the relative velocities of ions very small currents must be employed, to avoid appreciable thermal changes, and in any wise mixing the solutions mechanically.

The next problem is *the effect of concentration of the solution* on the relative velocities. The more concentrated the solution the greater the viscosity, and, consequently, the greater the resistance offered to the movement of the ions through it. It seems probable that the movements of different ions would be affected differently, depending upon their size, mass, etc.

Hittorf has also experimented on this part of the problem, using solutions of copper sulphate ranging in concentration from one to twenty-four, and very different relative velocities were found for the copper ion. A few of his results with copper sulphate are as follows:

Parts Water to One Part Copper Sulphate	Relative Velocity of Copper.
6 35	0 276
18.08	0.326
76.98	0.349
148.30	0.262

The velocity of copper as compared with the SO_4 ion is not constant, but increases with the dilution up to a certain point, beyond which it was found to remain constant no matter how much farther the dilution was increased.

The following are a few of the results which were obtained with silver nitrate:

Parts Water to One Part Silver Nitrate.	Velocity of the Silver Ion.
2.49	0.532
14 50	0 475
247.30	0.476

As the dilution of the solution increases the velocity of the silver ion decreases up to a certain point, and then remains constant, no matter how much farther the dilution is carried.

In determining the relative velocities of ions it is, therefore, necessary to use very dilute solutions, and, indeed, solutions which are so dilute that when the dilution is increased still farther the relative velocities do not change. This point must be carefully observed in all work in which the relative velocities of ions are concerned.

The effect of *temperature* on the relative velocities of ions has also been made a matter of experiment. It is difficult to say just what result we should expect in this case. Perhaps, if temperature has any influence we would expect it to increase the difference between the velocities of the two ions, accelerating the faster ion at the expense of the slower. Hittorf, who worked on this problem over a considerable range of temperature, concluded that temperature has no effect on the relative velocities of the ions in copper sulphate.

Subsequent work, and especially that of Nernst on solutions of silver salts, has shown that his conclusion is erroneous. His results are extremely interesting, in that with *increase in temperature the velocities of all ions tend to become the same*.

Still more recent work by Bein, in Berlin, has shown that this conclusion is probably correct. A few of Bein's results are given below:

TEMPERATURES.

	20 Degrees.	90 Degrees.
Sodium chloride	0.608	0 551
Calcium "	0.602	0.549
Silver nitrate	0.470	0.490

The velocities given are those of the anions, and show that increase in temperature slows up the faster ion and accelerates the slower.

The meaning of this fact we do not know at present, but it is certainly very significant.

THE RESULTS FOR THE MORE COMMON IONS.

The relative velocities of some of the more common ions, expressed in the same units, as taken from the best measurements thus far made, are the following:

$$\overset{+}{H} = 325 \qquad \tfrac{1}{2}\overset{++}{Cd} = 55$$

$$\overset{--}{OH} = 170 \qquad \tfrac{1}{2}\overset{++}{Ca} = 62$$

$$\overset{+}{K} = 70.6 \qquad \tfrac{1}{2}\overset{++}{Sr} = 63$$

$$\overset{+}{Na} = 49.2 \qquad \overset{-}{Cl} = 70.2$$

$\overset{+}{Ag} = 59.1 \qquad \overset{-}{Br} = 73.0$

$\tfrac{1}{2}\overset{++}{Cu} = 59.0 \qquad \overset{-}{I} = 72.0$

$\tfrac{1}{2}\overset{++}{Zn} = 54.0 \qquad \overset{-}{NO_3} = 65.1$

Hydrogen is much the swiftest of all the ions, having a velocity which is nearly twice that of the next swiftest ion—hydroxyl. Hydroxyl, in turn, has a velocity which is more than twice as great as the next faster ion; and, then, the velocities of the more common ions are of the magnitudes given in the table.

Our attention is naturally attracted in this connection especially to the two ions hydrogen and hydroxyl; these moving so much faster than any other known substances. A moment's thought and we see that these are the ions which, when combined, form water; and they are the ions formed when water dissociates. This recalls the *remarkable properties in general of the substance, water.* If we compare almost any property of water with the corresponding property of other substances, we shall find that it represents an extreme value. It either stands at the head or at the bottom of the list with re-

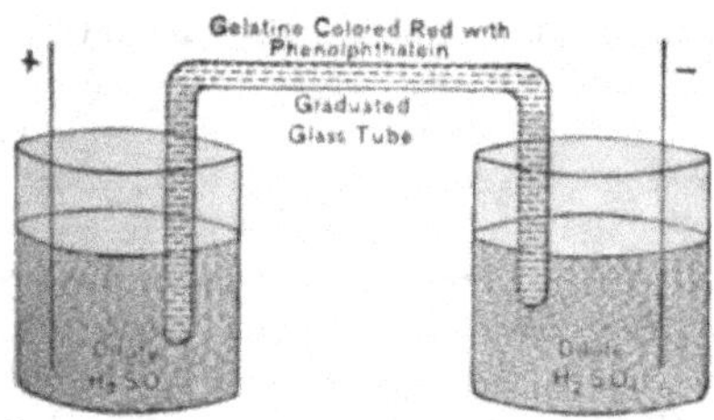

Fig. 6.—Diagramatic Sketch of Apparatus for Determining Absolute Velocities of Ions.

spect to a given property, and usually at the head. Take the specific heat of liquids, water stands at the top. Take the dielectric constants or specific inductive capacities of liquids, water again stands at the top; with

the possible exception of hydrogen dioxide, which, however, has not been proved. Take the power of liquids to dissolve other substances, water is by far the best solvent known. Take the power of solvents to ionize electrolytes, water is the strongest dissociant known; and so it goes through the long list of properties which can be compared. Taking all in all, the result of such a comparison would inevitably lead to the conclusion that *water is by far the most remarkable chemical compound known to man.*

The above is a slight digression from the main theme, but was suggested by the incomparably great velocities of the ions which unite and form water, and into which water dissociates, if only slightly, under ordinary conditions.

THE RELATIVE VELOCITIES OF ELEMENTARY IONS A PERIODIC FUNCTION OF THE ATOMIC WEIGHT.

We know to-day that a great number of the properties of the elements are periodic functions of the atomic weights of these elements. These relations have been generalized in the well-known "Periodic system" of the elements, which applies not only to the chemical, but also to the physical properties of these elementary substances. Ostwald and Bredig have pointed out that this same periodicity manifests itself in the relative velocities of the ions. If these are plotted as ordinates against the atomic weights as abscissas, the halogens fall very near the maxima of the curve. The alkali metals occupy nearly the same position, while at the minima we find chromium and aluminum. Calcium and the other alkaline earths, barium, strontium, and magnesium, occur at breaks on the descending arms of the curve, while cadmium and zinc occur near the minima.

While we have no idea as to the meaning of this recurrence of properties as the atomic weights increase, it is certainly of more than ordinary interest.

THE ABSOLUTE VELOCITIES OF IONS.

We have had to do thus far entirely with the relative velocities with which the ions move. This gives us, of course, no clue whatsoever as to the absolute distances which the ions travel in a given time under a given driving force.

Two general methods of determining the absolute velocities of ions have been worked out. Only one of these will be considered here. This involves a direct measurement of the distance traveled by a given ion in a given time, under a given potential gradient. The method in question was devised by the English physicist, Lodge, whose name it bears.

A graduated glass tube was bent at right angles near both ends, and filled with an aqueous solution of gelatine, to which some sodium chloride had been added. The contents of the tube were colored red by phenolphthaleïn, to which just enough sodium hydroxide had been added to bring out the red color. Both ends of this glass tube dip into vessels containing a dilute solution of sulphuric acid. Electrodes are inserted into these vessels, and a current passed from one to the other through the graduated glass tube. The hydrogen ions pass with the current into the graduated tube, displace the sodium ions from the sodium chloride, forming hydrochloric acid which decolorizes the phenolphthaleïn. The time is noted during which the current flows, the distance which the hydrogen ions travel is measured, and the drop in potential between the poles, which gives the potential gradient when the distance is known, is deter-

mined, and we have the data necessary for calculating the absolute velocities with which the ions travel under the potential gradient in question.

The unit potential gradient is taken as a drop of a volt a centimetre, and for this gradient Lodge found the velocity of hydrogen, the swiftest of all ions, to be in round numbers three thousandths of a centimetre per second. In three determinations he obtained these values:

```
0.0029 cm. per second.
0 0026  "    "    "
0.0024  "    "    "
```

Knowing the absolute velocity of one ion, and the relative velocities of all the more common ions, we can calculate at once the absolute velocities of all of these ions for unit potential gradient.

The above results for the velocity of hydrogen, the swiftest of all ions, cannot but impress us by their small magnitude. Perhaps, however, we should not be surprised after all at these figures, when we consider the enormous resistance offered to the movements of the ions by the presence of the solvent, which always has considerable viscosity. The comparatively free movements of the gaseous molecules through space cannot be compared with the movements of the ions through the resistent solvents, and yet we are tempted to try such comparisons, since the laws of gas-pressure apply to the osmotic pressure of solutions. It seems pretty clear that the cause of gas-pressure is to be found in the impacts of the rapidly moving gaseous particles against the walls of the confining vessel. It is difficult to furnish any similar explanation of osmotic pressure, especially when we consider how slowly the ions move through the solvent, even under a considerable driving force. That the molecules move with extreme slowness through the solvent is shown by the enormous amount of time required for diffusion to establish equilibrium in solutions, as became obvious when we were considering the principle of Soret. In the light of all these facts, and of the many unsuccessful attempts which have been made to explain osmotic pressure, it is only fair to say that we do not know what is the cause of osmotic pressure, but we do know very much about its results and their analogies to gas-pressure, the importance of which will appear before this series of papers is concluded.

A method for determining the absolute velocities of certain ions, based upon the same general principle as that of Lodge, was devised by Whetham in England. The method is so simple and yields such good results that it should be considered in this connection. The apparatus used consists of a longer perpendicular glass arm, with a shorter arm attached obliquely to one side. One electrode is introduced into each arm. In order that this method should be applied, it is necessary to have a common ion in combination with two other ions, the one colorless and the other colored. Thus, we must have chlorine in combination with copper; *i. e.*, a solution of copper chloride, and also chlorine in combination with some colorless ion like ammonium; *i. e.*, a solution of ammonium chloride. The denser solution (copper chloride) is poured into the longer arm of the apparatus until it rises a certain distance into the shorter arm, and the lighter solution (ammonium chloride) is carefully poured on to the top of the denser solution in the shorter arm. The current is now passed through the solutions from the ammonium to the copper chloride. The copper ions, like the ammonium, move with the current, and since

they are colored and give the color to the solution of cupric chloride, the bounding layer between the two solutions, as it moves with the current, can be seen.

The time during which the current passed was noted, also the potential gradient of the current, and the distance traveled by the bounding layer between the two solutions. From these data the abso-

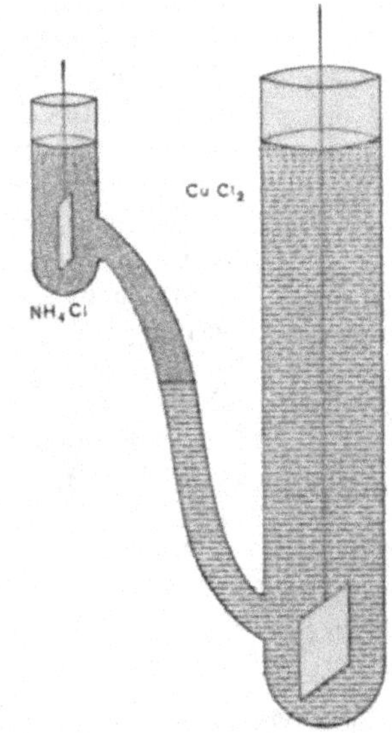

FIG. 7.—APPARATUS FOR WHETHAM'S METHOD OF DETERMINING VELOCITY OF IONS.

lute velocity of the copper ion in centimetres per second could be at once calculated.

This method is, of course, limited in its applicability to cases similar to the above, where the movement of the ion in question can be traced by means of changes in color.

In the last few years there have been a number of investigations*· along the

---

* These will all be cited in the paper which will soon appear, by Mather, in the *American Chemical Journal.*

lines indicated in this paper, but the principles involved are essentially the same as those already considered. These investigations have had to do chiefly with improvements in the form of apparatus used, and in effecting better separations of the solutions after the electrolysis was completed. They will, therefore, not be further considered in this paper.

THE NATURE OF THE IONS.

The method of electrolyzing solutions, which we have just been considering in connection with the determination of the relative velocity of ions, is also of value as enabling us to determine which constituents form cations and which anions. In the great majority of cases there is no difficulty encountered in answering this question. We know that all acids dissociate into a hydrogen cation, which gives them their characteristic property, and into an anion which comprises all the remainder of the molecule, and which, of course, varies with every acid. The general scheme of dissociation which is followed by acids is the following:

$$RH = \bar{R} + \overset{+}{H}.$$

Where $\bar{R}$ comprises all the molecule except the so-called replaceable hydrogen.

In the case of polybasic acids, the process is more complicated. Sulphuric acid breaks down first into $\overset{=}{HSO_4}$ and $\overset{+}{H}$ and then, as the dilution is increased, the complex anion $\overline{HSO_4}$ breaks down into $\overset{=}{SO_4}$ and $\overset{+}{H}$.

The dissociation of bases is just as simple as that of acids, univalent bases dissociating according to the following scheme:

$$R'OH = \overset{+}{R'} + \overline{OH}.$$

The hydroxyl anion is the characteristic ion of all bases, and the remainder of the molecule forms the cation $\overset{+}{R'}$. Polyacid bases, like polybasic acids, may break down in stages, and in the cases of some of the weak bases almost certainly do so.

In connection with acids and bases it should be stated that some compounds dissociate under one set of conditions as an acid, and under other conditions as a base. Thus, aluminum hydroxide in the presence of a strong acid dissociates as a base, forming a salt with the acid; while in the presence of a strong base it dissociates as an acid, forming a salt with the base.

The general scheme according to which salts of simple acids with simple bases dissociate is;

$$RR' = \bar{R} + \overset{+}{R'},$$

in which $\bar{R}$ is the anion of the acid and $\overset{+}{R'}$ the cation of the base. But either $\bar{R}$ or $\overset{+}{R'}$, or both, may be very complex, and in these cases it is often difficult to say just how the salt will dissociate. In such doubtful cases the method of electrolysis comes to our aid. Take the compound potassium platinic chloride, K_2PtCl_4: how will it dissociate in the presence of water? It is quite probable, indeed, almost certain, that the more strongly positive potassium will exist in the cationic condition; but how about the platinum? will it also form cations or will it form a part of the anion? This can be answered by electrolyzing a solution of the compound, and then determining by analysis whether the platinum goes to the cathode or to the anode. It goes to the anode, forming a part of the anion, and the compound, therefore, dissociates as follows:

$$K_2PtCl_6 = \overset{+}{K} + \overset{+}{K} + \overset{=}{PtCl_6}.$$

Take another case, potassium ferrocyanide $K_4Fe(CN)_6$; the potassium would obviously form cations, but what about the iron, would it also form cations, or would it, like the platinum in the above example, form part of the anion? The electrolysis of a solution of this salt in vessels like those already described in this chapter, in which the solutions can be readily separated after the electrolysis is ended, would answer the question. The   has been found to go to the anode, and,   forms part of the anion.

Other cases, considerably more complicated than the above, have been dealt with, in which the less positive metal went partly with the current to the cathode, and partly against the current to the anode, showing that it partly dissociated as cation and partly as anion. The above examples, however, suffice to illustrate the manner in which electrolysis is made use of to determine how any given compound dissociates, and what is the nature of the cation and what that of the anion.

In the next chapter we shall study the passage of the current through solutions of electrolytes, or the conductivity of solutions.

CHAPTER VI—CONDUCTIVITY OF SOLUTIONS.

REFERENCE has been frequently made in the preceding chapters, to the passage of electricity through solutions of certain substances. Indeed, the whole process of electrolysis depends upon the passage of the current through such solutions. We have also learned that chemical substances differ greatly in their power to carry the current; the acids, bases, and salts, forming the class known as electrolytes, being conductors, while all other chemical compounds fall into the class of non-conductors, and do not carry the current through their solutions. We thus have all chemical compounds dividing themselves into two great classes with respect to the property of conducting the current. Again, we shall see that among the electrolytes there are marked differences, some conducting to a much greater extent under the same conditions than others. We must now study in some detail the conducting power of solutions of electrolytes.

SPECIFIC AND MOLECULAR CONDUCTIVITIES.

The conducting power of any conducting substance depends not only upon the nature of the substance, but upon its form and dimensions. In order that we may compare the conductivities of different substances we must, therefore, use pieces of the same form and the same dimensions. The form chosen and the unit of dimensions selected are purely arbitrary. In studying the conductivities of substances, or their reciprocal the resistances, as is well known two units have been selected, the one a cube whose edge is a centimetre in length, and the other a cylinder one metre long and one square millimetre in cross-section. The resistance of the latter unit of form and dimensions for any given substance is obviously ten thousand times the former, or the conductivity is one ten-thousandth of the former. The resistance of these units of any substance is known as the *specific resistance of the substance;* the reciprocal of the specific resistance being the *specific conductivity.*

These terms as applied above hold for solid conductors, such as pieces of metal, carbon, etc. The question arises how can we apply them to conductors of the second class, or dissolved electrolytes? Since the conductivities of solutions are due entirely to the dissolved electrolytes, we must deal with comparable quantities of these substances in order that the results may be comparable. We might choose any quantity of an electrolyte as our unit, but it is most convenient here, and in most other cases, to work with quantities which bear the same relations to one another as the molecular weights of the substances in question; *i. e.,* to use gram-molecular weights of the different electrolytes.

Let us take a litre of a normal solution of an electrolyte; *i. e.,* a solution containing a gram-molecular weight of the electrolyte in a litre, and place it between the electrodes one centimetre apart. The conductivity of this solution would be, obviously, one thousand times that of a cube of this solution whose edge was a centimetre in length.

If we make this general, and represent

by n the number of cubic centimetres of a solution which contains a gram-molecular weight of the electrolyte, and by s the specific conductivity of a cube of this solution whose edge is a centimetre in length, the molecular conductivity m would be expressed thus:

$$m = n\,s.$$

If, on the other hand, we represent by the specific conductivity s, that of a cylinder of the solution one metre in length and one square millimetre in cross-section, the molecular conductivity would be calculated from the specific as follows:.

$$m = 10,000\,n\,s.$$

For a normal solution $n = 1,000$, hence,

$$m = s \times 10,000 \times 1,000$$
$$= s \times 10^7$$

The *molecular conductivity* is equal to the specific conductivity referred to the cubital unit multiple by 10^3, or to the specific conductivity referred to the cylinder unit multiplied by 10^7. Given either the specific or molecular conductivity it is a very simple matter to transform it into the other.

THE KOHLRAUSCH METHOD OF MEASURING THE CONDUCTIVITY OF SOLUTIONS.

A large number of methods have been devised in the last quarter of a century for measuring the conductivity of solutions, but all of these have been practically supplanted by the method of F. Kohlrausch. When a continuous current is passed through a solution of any electrolyte, gas is evolved on one or both poles, and the latter become, as we say, polarized. This would evidently increase the resistance to the passage of the current, and must be avoided. To avoid this Kohlrausch used an alternating current, which was obtained from a small induction coil, and passed this between platinum electrodes immersed in the solution. The method of Kohlrausch consists in balancing the resistance of the solution, which is the quantity to be measured, against a standard rheostat, and determining when the balance is effected by means of a Wheatstone bridge. This method will be easily understood by means of the following diagram:

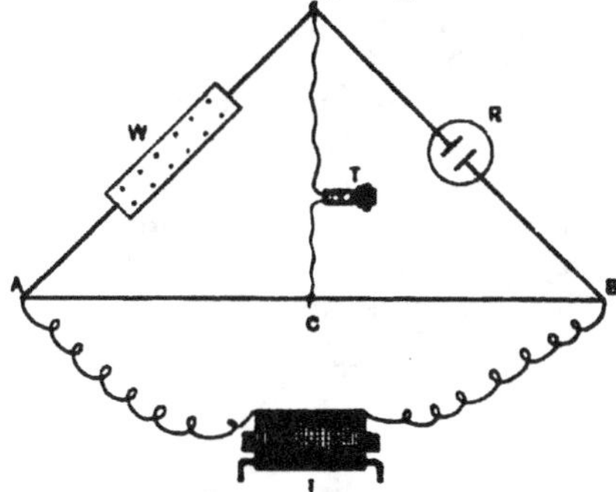

FIG 8.—DIAGRAM OF CONDUCTIVITY APPARATUS.

I is a small induction coil, which sends an alternating current through the bridge, AB, and also through the resistance box W, and the vessel containing the solution, R. The second circuit of the current is connected with the first through the bridge by means of the telephone, T. When the resistance in the rheostat, W, is exactly equal to the resistance in the solution in R, and C is just half-way between A and B, no current will flow through the telephone, and, consequently, the sound of the induction coil will not be heard in the telephone. The wire from the telephone connects with the bridge at C by means of a slider, so that this connection can be moved along the wire.

It is not necessary that the resistance of the solution should be exactly equalized by the resistance thrown into the box. In this case the point of silence would not fall in the centre of the bridge, but this is of no consequence, since it is only necessary to move C along the wire until equilibrium is reached, which is shown by the disappearance of the sound of the coil in the telephone.

In this and all other cases the calculation of the resistance in ohms offered by the solution is a very simple matter, using the principle of the Wheatstone bridge. The conductivity is but the reciprocal of the resistance. If we represent AC by a, and BC by b, the resistance in W by w, and the resistance of the solution in the cup by r, applying the principle of the Wheatstone bridge, we would have:

$$ra = wb,$$
or
$$r = \frac{wb}{a}.$$

Since the conductivity, c, of a solution is the reciprocal of its resistance, we have:

$$c = \frac{a}{wb}.$$

The conductivities of solutions calculated from this expression would not be comparable with each other, since it contains no term which has to do with the concentration of the solution. It is very convenient to refer all concentrations to molecular normal, which contains a gram-molecular weight of the electrolyte in a litre of solution. If we represent the number of litres of the solution which contains a gram-molecular weight of the electrolyte by v, the above equation becomes,

$$c = \frac{va}{wb}.$$

We now write for the molecular conductivity the letter μ; and indicating the concentration at which μ is determined by v, we write μ_v.

$$\mu_v = \frac{va}{wb}.$$

This expression, however, does not take into account the dimensions of the cell. A cell constant, k, must be introduced for each cell and determined before the cell can be used for conductivity measurements. The complete equation for the molecular conductivity μ_v is then:

$$\mu_v = k\,\frac{va}{wb}.$$

In actually carrying out a conductivity measurement, a large number of factors come into play, and many conditions must be observed. The *cell constant, k,* must first be determined by using some substance whose molecular conductivity for a given dilution and temperature is known. The *wire must be calibrated,* and corresponding corrections applied. *Water must be especially purified* for all conductivity work, and the conductivity of the water used in preparing the solutions must always be determined. These and many other conditions must be observed, but space will not permit of a further discussion of these details in this connection. If it is desired to apply the above method, reference must be had to some of the works* which deal with this question in detail.

The *effect of temperature* on the conductivity of solutions is so pronounced and of such a nature that it cannot be passed over with a mere reference. The conductivity of a metallic wire decreases with increase in temperature. As the

---

* For details in carrying out a conductivity measurement, see works by Ostwald and Kohlrausch, and also Freezing-point, Boiling point and Conductivity measurements by Jones. (Chemical Publishing Company, Easton.)

temperature of a piece of metal is lowered its conductivity increases, until at absolute zero the conductivity would become infinite, or the resistance zero.

With conductors of the second class, as solutions, the temperature coefficient has exactly the opposite sign. As the temperature is raised the conductivity increases, and very rapidly. That is, the temperature coefficient is positive for solutions of electrolytes, and very large. The magnitude can be seen from the following experimental facts: The molecular conductivity of a normal solution of hydrochloric acid at 18 degrees is 280; at 50 degrees, it is 404; at 80 degrees, it is 519, while at 100 degrees, it is 590.

In carrying out measurements of conductivity it is, therefore, necessary to keep the temperature constant to within very narrow limits, and for this purpose a number of thermo-regulators and thermostats have been devised and used. Here, again, for details reference must be had to some of the works which deal exhaustively with this subject.

RESULTS OF THE MEASUREMENTS OF THE CONDUCTIVITIES OF SOLUTIONS.

As quickly as the conductivities of substances in solution began to be studied, the two great divisions into which all chemical compounds fall were discovered. We have those substances like cane sugar, dextrose, the alcohols, ethers, ketones, and, in general, the great body of neutral organic compounds, whose solutions are no better conductors of the current than pure water. These non-electrolytes include, roughly speaking, perhaps half of the chemical compounds known.

We have, on the other hand, those substances whose solutions conduct the current, known as electrolytes. These include all the acids, all the bases, and all the salts of strong acids with strong bases, or of weak acids with weak bases. We find in this class something like half of the chemical compounds known. If we come to examine more closely the electrolytes themselves, we find marked differences between the conducting powers of different members of this class. The best conductors are the strong mineral acids like hydrochloric, nitric, hydrobromic, etc. Next in order come the strong bases, including those of the alkali and alkaline earth metals, such as potassium and sodium hydroxides, calcium, barium, and strontium hydroxides, but not ammonium hydroxide, which is a poor conductor. Finally, among the good conductors of the current when in solution are the salts in general; but within this class marked differences exist. All the ordinary salts are good conductors, though not as good as the bases, and still less than the acids, but the salts of a few metals like cadmium and mercury are in general only fair conductors of electricity, and some of the salts of these two metals, such as the halides, cyanides, etc., are really to be ranked among the poor conductors.

The above are the good conductors of electricity in solutions. We find, however, among the electrolytes, nearly all grades of conductivity represented. Among the organic acids and bases some are quite good conductors, like formic and oxalic acids, and the substituted ammonias, while acetic and hydrocyanic acids, and ammonia are among the very poor conductors.

It might be thought from this that there are all grades of conductivity represented, and that the distinction between electrolytes and non-electrolytes is not a sharp one. It is true that among the electrolytes nearly all grades of conductivity are represented, but there is a sharp distinction between those substances which have any conductivity and those which have none, and this is the line of division between the electrolytes and the non-electrolytes.

AN EXPERIMENTAL DEMONSTRATION OF THE DIFFERENT CONDUCTING POWERS OF DIFFERENT SUBSTANCES

has been furnished by Noyes and Blanchard,* and which they say was devised by Whitney. Half-normal solutions of hydrochloric, sulphuric, chloracetic, and acetic acids were prepared, and an equal volume of each introduced into a glass tube about 20 cm. long and 3 cm. internal diameter, which already contained a measured volume of water. Glass tubes carrying copper wires pass into these tubes through rubber stoppers, the wires terminating in platinum plates which are placed horizontally and dip into the solutions. These glass tubes can be readily shoved up and down through the rubber stoppers which close the tops of the large glass tubes, so that the platinum plate can be placed at any desired position in the glass tube. The wire from the bottom of each tube, connecting with a second electrode, passes through a 110-volt, 32-candle-power lamp, the other side of each lamp being connected with one wire from a 110-volt alternating-current dynomo. The other wire from the dynamo connects with the wires leading into the tops of the four glass tubes.

The authors recommend that 100 cubic centimetres of water, and 5 cubic centimetres of one of the solutions be added to each tube. After the solu-

* *Jour. Amer. Chem. Soc.*, xxii, 736.

tions in the tubes have become homogeneous, the current is closed and the positions of the electrodes so adjusted in the four tubes that the lamps are all equally bright. If the electrode in the hydrochloric acid is placed at the top of the tube, that in the sulphuric acid will be about one-fourth from the top, that in the chloracetic acid will be about three-fourths from the top, while in the solution of acetic acid the movable electrode will nearly touch the electrode placed at the bottom of the tube. These distances between the electrodes in the four tubes show the rela-

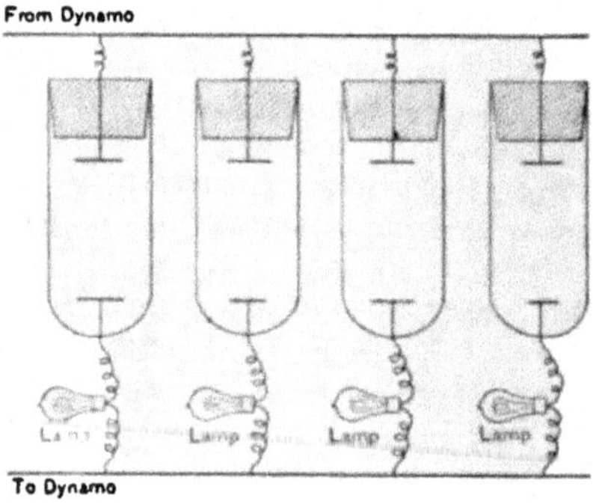

FIG. 9.—APPARATUS FOR SHOWING DIFFERENCES IN CONDUCTING POWER.

tive conductivities of the four substances. Hydrochloric acid is the best conductor, since an equal amount of current passes through it when the electrodes are the farthest apart; sulphuric acid comes next, requiring the electrodes to be somewhat closer in order that the same amount of current may pass; chloracetic acid next, and then acetic acid, which is such a poor conductor that the electrodes must be very near together in order that the given amount of current may pass.

The authors also point out that this experiment can be used to illustrate another point. If we just neutralize the acid in each cylinder with a base and form the corresponding salt, and then repeat the above experiment, we shall find that when the lights are all equally brilliant the electrodes in the four cylinders are equally distant apart. This shows that while the four acids have very different conducting powers, their salts with a given base are equally good conductors.

KOHLRAUSCH'S LAW OF CONDUCTIVITY.

If we study the conductivity of any given electrolyte—say a strong acid—we would find that the molecular conductivity increases as the dilution of the solution increases. This means that the actual resistance of the solution does not increase as rapidly as the dilution of the solution. This increase in the conductivity with the dilution goes on until a certain dilution is reached, and beyond this point the molecular conductivity does not further increase, but remains constant. The dilution at which the molecular conductivities of the strongly dissociated electrolytes become constant is about 1,000 litres; *i. e.*, 1,000 litres of such a solution would contain a gram-molecular weight of the electrolyte.

If the electrolyte is a poor conductor, the same general remarks apply. The molecular conductivity increases with the dilution, and continues to increase even at very great dilutions. Indeed, if the compound in question is such a poor conductor as ammonia or acetic acid, the molecular conductivity will increase with the dilution, even at the greatest dilutions to which the conductivity method can be applied. In such cases the maximum constant value of the molecular conductivity cannot be obtained by direct application of the conductivity method, but some indirect method must be employed.

This maximum constant value of the molecular conductivity for any substance has been given a specific name. It is known as the μ_∞ for the substance. It is between the values of μ_∞ for different substances that Kohlrausch discovered a generalization of wide-reaching importance. Comparing the values of μ_∞ for different electrolytes containing a common ion, he obtained such results as these:

Potassium chloride, μ_∞ at 18° = 121.7
Sodium   "   "   " = 102.4

              Difference = 19.3
Potassium bromide, μ at 18° = 141.0
Sodium   "   "   " = 121.0

              Difference = 20.0

Such relations are general. The difference between the values of μ_∞ for any two compounds containing a common ion combined with two different ions, is the same as the difference between the values of μ_∞ for any other two compounds containing these same different ions combined with any other common ion.

In order that this may be true the *value of μ_∞ must be made up of two constants,* the one depending upon the anion and the other upon the cation. If we represent these constants by a and c, respectively, the above relation would be formulated thus:

$$\mu_\infty = a + c.$$

Since the conductivity of a solution depends upon the number of ions present and the velocities with which they move, and since the value of μ_∞ has to do with complete dissociation of comparable quantities of substances and, therefore, with the same number of ions, its value depends upon the velocities with which the ions move. The *two constants, a and c, in the above equation are, then, proportional to the velocities* $_{o}$*f the anion and cation, respectively.*

The above law is generally known as the law of the independent migration velocities of the ions, each ion moving with a velocity which is independent of the nature of the other ion or ions with which it is associated in the solution.

THE VELOCITY OF IONS DETERMINED BY MEANS OF THE LAW OF KOHLRAUSCH.

In the preceding chapter we discussed methods for determining relative velocities of ions in general, and methods for determining the absolute velocities of a few ions. The law of Kohlrausch opens up new possibilities in the field of ionic velocities, as we can readily see. The sum of a and c, as we have seen, is μ_{∞}, and a and c are either the velocities of the anions and cations, respectively, or are a multiple of these velocities, and it has been shown that they are the velocities of these ions. We thus have $a + c = \mu_{\infty}$. From the study of the relative velocities of ions we obtained the ratio of c to a. We then know $c + a$ and $\dfrac{c}{a}$ and can calculate at once the absolute velocities of the ions.

The velocities of the ions, as thus determined, using Kohlrausch's law, agree very well with the results obtained by the methods described in the preceding chapter, as far as the results for the same ions have been determined by the different methods. The law of Kohlrausch is, then, undoubtedly correct, and greatly simplifies the whole problem of the conductivity of solutions.

Suppose it is desired to determine the velocities of the complex anions into which

the organic acids dissociate. It wa impossible to determine directly the of μ_{∞} for these acids, since they slightly dissociated that μ_{∞} wou reached only at such great dilution the conductivity method would r applicable to them. Some salts of acids would be prepared, say the s salt, which is completely dissociate at moderate dilutions. The value for the sodium salt would be deter from this the constant for sodium be subtracted, and the remainder be the constant or velocity of the an question. The first question which naturally arise would be; what would the composition of the ion h its velocity? As we would expect, found that the more *complex* the i *less* its velocity.

The effect of the chemical consti of the ion on its velocity was also st and it was shown by studying is ions, which have the same comp but different constitution, that co tion has very little influence on the ity of complex organic anions.

The velocities of the complex cati organic bases were studied by me Kohlrausch's law, in a manner a analogous to that just described f complex anions of organic acids. value of μ_{∞} for the poorly cond base could not be determined direc the conductivity method, and a salt base which would be strongly disso was prepared and the value of the salt ascertained. If the chlor the base was used the constant for rine was subtracted from the value for the salt, and the remainder, Kohlrausch's law, is the velocity cation of the base. Similar results

ed by Bredig for the velocities of
mplex cations of organic bases, as
een obtained by Ostwald for the
ex anions of organic acids.

ONDUCTIVITY OF ELECTROLYTES AS A
EASURE OF THEIR DISSOCIATION.

have constantly referred to the
iation of electrolytes in solution,
ave pointed out one convenient
d, based upon the lowering of
reezing point of solvents by dis-
substances, for measuring the
it of dissociation. The conduc-
of electrolytes furnishes us with
r, and perhaps still more convenient
d for measuring dissociation. The
ple upon which the method is based
y simple. If the substance is not
iated, the solution would have no
ctivity at all, as is shown by solu-
of non-electrolytes, which do not
ct the current to $e_v e_n$ a slight ex-
This shows that molecules have no
to carry the current, since in solu-
of non-electrolytes there is an abun-
of molecules and yet no con-
ity.
have seen that the molecular con-
ity increases with the dilution up to
ain point, where it attains a maxi-
constant value. This means that
molecules have broken down into
When there is no dissociation there
m, no conductivity; where dissocia-
s complete the conductivity is a
num. If the molecular conductivity
ewhere between zero and a maxi-
value, the dissociation is partial;
between zero per cent and 100 per

m the conductivity results it is, then,
a matter of proportion to calculate

the amount of dissociation of the electrolyte. It is only necessary to divide the
molecular conductivity at the dilution in
question, by the maximum molecular con-
is complete, in order to obtain the percentage of the dissociation of the electrolyte at
the dilution with which we are dealing. If
we represent the molecular conductivity at
a given dilution by μ_v, and the maximum molecular conductivity for complete
dissociation by μ_∞, the percentage of
dissociation a, is obtained thus :

$$a = \frac{\mu_v}{\mu_\infty}.$$

To measure dissociation by the conductivity method, it is only necessary, then, to
determine the molecular conductivity of
the substance at the given dilution whose
volume is v, and the maximum molecular
conductivity of the substance.

The first part of this problem is always
very simple, involving only the determination of conductivity in the usual way.
The second part, involving the determination of μ_∞, is not always so simple a
matter. If the electrolyte is strongly dissociated the determination of μ_∞ presents no serious difficulties. It is only
necessary to increase the dilution step by
step, measuring the conductivity at each
dilution, until the molecular conductivity
has acquired a maximum, constant, value.
This is the value of μ_∞. For the more
strongly dissociated electrolytes, this value
is reached at a dilution of about 1,000
litres in water as a solvent, and at this
dilution there is no serious difficulty in
making a conductivity measurement by
the Kohlrausch method, if the electrodes
in the resistance vessel are placed close together. For these high dilutions, where

the resistance of the solution has become quite large, the plates should be placed close together in order that the resistance which must be thrown into the box to effect a balance near the centre of the bridge, may not be too large. If the resistance is very great the tone-minima in the telephone are not sharp. If, on the other hand, we are working with fairly concentrated solutions, whose resistance is small, the plates must be close together in order that an appreciable resistance may be thrown into the box to bring the balance near the centre of the bridge; since a sharp tone-minimum is not obtained when the resistance in the circuit is too small.

Difficulties in determining μ_∞ arise only in the cases of weakly dissociated electrolytes. In such cases the dissociation is not complete, even at a dilution of 10,000 litres, and at greater dilutions the conductivity method is not applicable with even a fair degree of accuracy. With weakly dissociated electrolytes it is, therefore, not possible to determine μ_∞ by the method employed with strongly dissociated substances; *i. e.*, by increasing the dilution step by step and measuring the molecular conductivity at each dilution until it reaches a maximum constant value. Some other method of determining μ_∞ for weakly dissociated compounds must be employed, or the conductivity method could not be used to measure the dissociation of these substances.

An indirect method of arriving at the values of μ_∞ for weakly dissociated compounds has, however, been worked out on the basis of the law of Kohlrausch. While the organic acids and bases are weakly dissociated compounds, the salts of these substances, like salts in general, are strongly dissociated. If we wish to determine the value of μ_∞ for a weak base like ammonium hydroxide, the salt of ammonia with some acid like hydrochloric is prepared, and the value of μ_∞ for ammonium chloride is ascertained in the usual manner, by increasing the dilution step by step until the molecular conductivity has attained a maximum, constant, value. From Kohlrausch's law, μ_∞ for ammonium chloride is made up of two constants, one depending upon the ammonium ion and the other upon the chlorine ion. If we subtract from the value of μ_∞ for ammonium chloride, the constant for chlorine, the remainder will be the constant for the cation ammonium. The value of μ_∞ for ammonium hydroxide is, from the law of Kohlrausch, the sum of the constants for the cation ammonium, and the anion hydroxyl. If, therefore, we add to the constant for ammonium, found as above described, the constant for hydroxyl, we have the values of μ_∞ for the weakly dissociated base ammonium hydroxide.

The procedure with weakly dissociated acids is strictly analogous to that just described for weakly dissociated bases. Suppose we wish to know the value of μ_∞ for acetic acid; this could not be determined directly for reasons already indicated. A salt of the acid with some base like potassium hydroxide is prepared, and the value of μ_∞ for potassium acetate determined in the usual manner. The constant for potassium is then subtracted from the value of μ_∞ for potassium acetate, and the remainder is the constant for the anion of acetic acid $CH_3\overline{COO}$. If to this constant we add the constant for the cation hydrogen, the sum is the value of μ_∞ for acetic acid

The conductivity method can thus be applied to measure the dissociation of weak acids and bases, as well as to measure the dissociation of strongly dissociated compounds.

We have, then, two general methods which can be conveniently applied to measure the dissociation of electrolytes—the conductivity method, and the freezing-point method. The question of importance which naturally arises is, how do the results obtained by these two methods agree when they are applied to the same solutions of the same substances?

The following comparison for a few compounds, taken from the conductivity measurements of Kohlrausch on the one hand, and from the freezing-point measurements of Jones, on the other, will answer this question.

	Concentration, Gram-Molec. Normal.	Dissociation from Freezing-Point Lowering.	Dissociation from Conductivity.
Hydrochloric acid	0.002	98 4 per cent.	100.0 per cent.
" "	0.01	95 8 "	98.9 "
" "	0.1	88.6 "	98 9 "
Potassium hydroxide	0.002	98.4 "	100.0 "
" "	0 01	98.7 "	99.2 "
" "	0.1	83.1 "	92.8 "
Sodium chloride	0.001	98 4 "	98.0 "
" "	0 01	90.5 "	98 5 "
" "	0.1	84.1 "	84.1 "

The agreement in a long series of comparisons is about as close as we could expect, under the different conditions under which the two sets of measurements were made.

CHAPTER VI–CONDUCTIVITY OF SOLUTIONS.

PART II.

THE DISSOCIATING POWER OF DIFFERENT SOLVENTS.*

We have dealt thus far in these papers exclusively with aqueous solutions, and the conclusion might be drawn that the theory of electrolytic dissociation applies only to solutions in water as the solvent. We shall now learn that such is by no means the case, since there are many solvents which have a marked dissociating power.

Water, to be sure, is the strongest dissociant known, breaking down electrolytes into ions to a greater extent than any other known substance, but there are other solvents which do not stand very far behind water in this respect. We shall take up first some inorganic solvents, then some organic solvents, and, finally, some mixtures of different solvents.

Liquid ammonia has been shown, especially by the work of Franklin and Kraus, to have a very considerable power as an ionizing solvent. Indeed, the molecular conductivities of certain electrolytes in liquid ammonia are greater than in water at the same concentration. This alone would not show that there is greater dissociation in the liquid ammonia than in water, since the measurements were made in the ammonia at its boiling-point, — 38 degrees, while the measurements were made in water at 18 degrees, or 82 degrees below its boiling-point. In order that the two sets of results should be comparable,

the molecular conductivities in water at its boiling-point should be compared with those in liquid ammonia at its boiling-point. Further, if the molecular conductivities in liquid ammonia should even prove to be greater, under comparable conditions, than in water, this alone would not show that ammonia has the greater dissociating power, since the dissociation a is the ratio between μ_v and μ_∞, and μ_v might be larger in ammonia than in water, and μ_∞ still larger in the ammonia. In this case a would be smaller in the ammonia. Such is, indeed, the fact; the greater molecular conductivity in the liquid ammonia being due rather to the great velocity with which the ions move through this solvent, than to the large number of ions present.

Nitric acid, in the liquid state, has been shown to have very great ionizing power. Indeed, from the few results thus far obtained it seems to have nearly as great dissociating power as water itself, but the data thus far available with this solvent are far too meagre to justify any final conclusion.

Sulphur dioxide, in the liquid condition, has been found by Walden to have a considerable dissociating power. Comparing the molecular conductivities of a number of salts in sulphur dioxide, with those for the same salts in water at 0 degrees, Walden concluded that liquid sulphur dioxide dissociates to from one-fourth to one-half the extent of water.

Of the organic solvents whose dissociating power is known, *formic* acid stands at

---

* This paragraph is taken from a review of the Dissociating Power of Solvents, recently prepared by H C Jones, and published in the *American Chemical Journal,* xxv, 282.

the head of the list. Quite an elaborate investigation on the dissociating power of formic acid was carried out by Zannino-vich-Tessarin. He used chiefly the freezing point method, but determined also the conductivity of a few salts in this solvent. He concluded that formic acid is one of the strongest dissociating solvents next to water. The behavior of hydrochloric acid in this solvent is most remarkable. Although it is one of the most strongly dissociated substances in water, it shows no dissociation whatever in formic acid, as measured by the freezing-point method. Indeed, in the latter solvent it is actually polymerized, according to the results obtained by this method. On the other hand, hydrochloric acid shows very marked conductivity in this solvent, indicating dissociation. This apparent discrepancy may be due to the fact, that while most of the molecules are polymerized into large complexes, some are dissociated into ions, which conduct the current.

Methyl alcohol, among the organic solvents, stands next to formic acid in its power to break down molecules into ions. A large number of investigators have worked on the conductivity of solutions of electrolytes in this solvent, but, on the whole, perhaps the work of Zelinsky and Krapiwin deserves special mention. Their work included a number of salts in pure methyl alcohol, as well as in a mixture of methyl alcohol and water. If the molecular conductivities in the methyl alcohol are compared with those in water at the same dilution, we would see that they are not very different. The conductivity in methyl alcohol is from two-thirds to three-fourths that in water, under the same conditions.

An examination of the conductivity results in methyl alcohol will show that it is almost impossible to reach the values of μ_∞ for the most strongly dissociated substances in this solvent. The dilution at which the electrolyte would be completely dissociated by this solvent, is so great that it is nearly impossible to apply the conductivity method to it, with even a fair degree of accuracy. It is, therefore, not possible to measure dissociation accurately in this solvent, by means of the conductivity method. The same remarks apply with even greater force to those solvents whose dissociating power is less than that of methyl alcohol. In such cases it is impossible to obtain the values of μ_∞ by the conductivity method, and, hence, the dissociation values obtained by this method can only be regarded as rough approximations. They are obtained by assuming that the values of μ in the solvent in question are the same as in water. An assumption which we know is not correct, since the friction offered by the different solvents to the movements of the ions is different, the velocities of the ions through these solvents would, therefore, be different, and the values of μ_∞ must be different. The above assumption is, however, the best that can be done under the conditions.

Another method of measuring dissociation has been applied by Jones to solvents like methyl alcohol. Attention has already been called to the lowering of the vapor-tension of solvents by dissolved substances. But lowering of vapor-tension is proportional to rise in boiling-point, and if we measure the rise in the boiling-points of solvents produced by dissolved substances, we can calculate the dissociation of the dissolved substances in exactly the same way, as we calculated the dissociation **of dissolved substances from the lowering** of the freezing-point of the solvent produced by them. Very satisfactory results **were obtained by the boiling-point method** for the dissociation of a number of salts in methyl alcohol, and the final conclusion was reached, as the result of this work, that the dissociation in methyl alcohol is, in round numbers, about two-thirds of that in water under the same conditions.

Ethyl alcohol has a much smaller dissociating power than methyl alcohol, as indicated by the conductivity method; but the dissociating power of this solvent can be measured only with very rough approximation by the conductivity method, on account of the impossibility of determining μ_∞.

The dissociation of a number of salts in ethyl alcohol has been measured by Jones, using the boiling-point method as with methyl alcohol. The results showed that the dissociating power of ethyl alcohol is from one-third to one-fourth that of water at the same dilution of the solutions.

The *more complex alcohols* dissociate much less than the simpler members of the series, as is indicated from the conductivity results, but for all slightly dissociating solvents the conductivity measurements must be taken as only very rough approximations, as a measure of dissociation. It has been found to be a general rule that, *in a homologous series of compounds the lower members have much higher ionizing power than the more complex members of the series.*

The conductivities of a number of electrolytes in *acetone and other ketones* have been measured, especially by Cattaneo, Carrara and St. Laszczynski. Such solutions have considerable conductivity, showing a marked ionization in these solvents. The ionizing power of the ketones in general decreases with increase in the complexity of the molecule.

The ionizing power of the *nitriles* has also been found to decrease with the complexity of the molecule.

The dissociating power of a number of other organic solvents has been studied. Solutions in ether, glycerol, chloroform, the hydrocarbons, and similar compounds, conduct very poorly. Some very surprising results have been obtained in *mixed solvents,* one example of which will be referred to. While electrolytes in methyl alcohol conduct the current very well, the conductivity is considerably less than in water. Zelinsky and Krapiwin found that certain salts have a greater conductivity in pure methly alcohol, than in a mixture of 50 per cent methyl alcohol and 50 per cent water. This is shown by the following results:

V is the volume of the solution, or the number of litres which contain a gram-molecular weight of the dissolved substance, and μ_v the molecular conductivity at volume v.

POTASSIUM BROMIDE.

v	Water. μ_v	Methyl Alcohol. μ_v	One-half Methyl Alcohol, One-half Water. μ_v
16	123.1	....	59.82
64	130.5	76.70	65.86
256	136.4	88.96	69.26
512	140.2	98.26	70.53

AMMONIUM IODIDE.

v	Water. μ_v	Methyl Alcohol. μ_v	One-half Methyl Alcohol One-half Water. μ_v
16	125.4	72.24	62.63
64	133.4	85.00	67.48
256	138.7	96.20	70.34
1024	143.7	104.70	71.57

It is impossible at present to say what these surprising and remarkable results mean. They have been confirmed by the work of others.

Similar results have been obtained by Cohen with mixtures of ethyl alcohol and water, but only when the mixture contained very little water, and when the dilution of the solution was quite great.

RELATIONS BETWEEN THE IONIZING POWER OF SOLVENTS AND OTHER PROPERTIES.

A number of attempts have been made to discover relations between the ionizing power and other properties of solvents. J. J. Thomson first proposed the theory, and a little later Nernst suggested the same idea, that there should be a close relation between the dissociating powers of solvents and their dielectric constants or specific inductive capacities. Those solvents which have the greatest dielectric constants undoubtedly have the greatest dissociating powers. With the possible exception of hydrogen dioxide, about which there is still some doubt, water has the highest dielectric constant, and also has the greatest dissociating power. Next to water comes formic acid, both with respect to dielectric constant and dissociating power. Of the more common organic solvents, methyl alcohol has the highest dielectric constant and also the greatest ionizing power. Ethyl alcohol has a considerably smaller dielectric constant and, as we have seen, much less power to break down molecules into ions.

Another suggestion, which we owe to Dutoit and Aston, is that the ionizing power of a solvent is closely connected with the state of aggregation of its own molecules; the greater the complexity of the molecules of any solvent the greater its power to break down molecules of dissolved substances into ions. We have a method of determining the complexity of molecules of liquids, based upon the measurement of their surface-tension. This method was devised and applied to a number of liquids by Ramsay and Shields some 10 years ago, with the result that many of the common solvents were found to consist of complex molecules. Thus, the molecules of the alcohols were, in general, made up of more than one of the simplest molecules, and water was found to be the most complex of all the liquids known. Its molecule consists of four of the simplest water molecules—$(H_2O)_4$. This most associated of all known liquids has the strongest ionizing power.

While there is undoubtedly an element of truth in both of these suggestions, they are far from an expression of the whole truth. These relations fail to hold, especially among the weakly dissociating solvents, where it is often impossible to say, either from the dielectric constants or from the degree of association, which of two solvents has the greater dissociating power. It will probably be shown that the dissociating power of a solvent is not a function of any one physical or chemical property of the substance, but of them all. Or, perhaps, more accurately expressed, all the properties of a substance are a function of the energy relations which obtain in that substance, and dissociating power is simply one of these properties. The conclusion from the study of the ionizing power of solvents, which is of greatest importance, is that ions are probably always present when chemical reaction takes place. When the number of solvents which can effect ionization is taken into account, and, further, that heat and possibly pressure can break molecules down into their ions, it will be seen that there is not a chemical reaction where the conditions for ion formation do not exist.

RELATION BETWEEN THE DILUTION OF SOLUTIONS AND THEIR DISSOCIATION.

It has already been pointed out that the percentage dissociation of solutions increases with the dilution, but while our knowledge was in this purely qualitative stage, we could scarcely hope to deduce any consequences of importance from it. A quantitative relation between dilution and dissociation has, however, been worked out by Ostwald; and has led to such important consequences that it must be carefully considered.

Ostwald[*] was impressed by the relation between an electrolyte undergoing dissociation into ions in the presence of a solvent like water, and a substance like ammonium chloride undergoing dissociation into the molecules, ammonia and hydrochloric acid, by heat. Since the laws of gas-pressure apply to the osmotic pressure of solutions, it seems probable that any deductions for the dissociation of a vapor by heat, would apply to the dissociation of an electrolyte by a solvent like water. Starting with this idea in mind Ostwald developed the following relations.

Given a vapor which is undergoing dissociation by heat, say that of ammonium chloride. If neither of the products of dissociation is present in excess, and if the temperature is maintained constant, the following relation obtains:

$$[\dagger]\;\text{``}\;\frac{p}{p_1{}^2} = \text{constant,} \qquad (1)$$

in which p is the pressure of the original gas, and p_1 that of the decomposition products. Turning now to solutions, we must deal with osmotic pressure instead of gas-pressure. The osmotic pressure is proportional to the amount of substance present, and inversely proportional to the volume. Let u be the mass of the undecomposed electrolyte, and u_1 the mass of the decomposition products; v is the volume:

$$p = \frac{u}{v} \text{ and } p_1 = \frac{u_1}{v}.$$

Substituting these values in (1), we have:

$$\frac{uv}{u_1{}^2} = \text{constant.} \qquad (2)$$

The amount of the dissociation products u_1, is equal to the relation between the conductivity at volume v, (μ_v), and the conductivity at infinite dilution (μ_∞),

$$u_1 = \frac{\mu_v}{\mu_\infty}.$$

The amount of the undissociated substance u, is the complement of u_1:

$$u = 1 - \frac{\mu_v}{\mu_\infty}.$$

Substituting these values of u and u_1 in (2) we have:

$$\frac{\mu_\infty\,(\mu_\infty - \mu_v)}{\mu_v{}^2}\, v = \text{constant,} \qquad (3)$$

and this is the dilution law of Ostwald. This can, however, be simplified. If we represent the activity coefficient, or the amount of dissociation, by a:

$$a = \frac{\mu_v}{\mu_\infty}.$$

Substituting this value in (3) we have:

$$\frac{a^2}{(1 - a)\,v} = \text{constant.} \qquad (4)\text{''}$$

So much for the mathematical deduction of the relation between these two kinds of dissociation. It now remains to see whether the deduction is correct, whether the conclusion is in accord with the facts. The way to test this is to take a solution of an electrolyte, and determine its dissociation by the conductivity or

---

[*] *Ztschr. phys. Chem*, ii, 184–276: iii, 170. See also Theory of Electrolytic Dissociation, p. 143.

[†] This paragraph is quoted from Theory of Electrolytic Dissociation, pp. 141–145.

freezing-point method; knowing the volume v, or the concentration of the solution, and having determined the dissociation a, we substitute these values in the above equation and calculate the value of the constant. We now dilute the solution still farther, and determine the value of a for the new dilution. Knowing v for the new dilution, and having determined a, we substitute these values in the above equation and calculate anew the value of the constant for this dilution. We proceed in exactly the same manner for a wide range of dilutions, and then see whether the values obtained for the constant are really constant or not, over a range of dilutions. Some of the results obtained for a few substances are given below:

ACETIC ACID.

v	a	Constant
8	1.193	0.00180
32	2.88	0.00188
256	6.56	0.00180
1024	12.66	0.00177

BUTYRIC ACID.

v	a	Constant.
8	1.068	0.00144
32	2.165	0.00149
256	5.988	0.00149
1024	11.41	0.00144

AMMONIA.

v	a	Constant.
8	1.36	0.0023
32	2.65	0.0018
128	5.33	0.0018
256	7.54	0.0004

TRIPHENYLMETHANE.

v	Constant.
8	0.0069
32	0.0078
64	0.0076
256	0.0074

The Ostwald dilution law deduced above, seems to hold fairly well for the above substances. Ostwald applied the law to more than two hundred organic acids, and Bredig applied it to a large number of organic bases; and it held satisfactorily for nearly all of these substances. The conclusion might be drawn from these facts that the law was of universal application, but it should be observed that the above compounds, organic acids and organic bases, are all weakly dissociated substances, as compared with inorganic substances. It might be that the law would hold for the weakly dissociated compounds, and not hold for the strongly dissociated acids, bases, and salts. This has, indeed, been found to be the case. The law of Ostwald does not hold for a single strongly dissociated substance.

The question is what is to be done? We have a dilution law for the weakly dissociated compounds, but we cannot discard the strongly dissociated compounds—the most important substances, by far, from a chemical standpoint. Fortunately, this is not necessary since the following discovery was made.

"Rudolphi,* from a study of the conductivity of solutions of silver nitrate of varying concentrations, discovered a new relation which obtains for the strongly dissociated compounds. If we represent the volume by v and the constant by c, as above, he found that when he applied the Ostwald equation to solutions of silver nitrate, he obtained the following values:

$$\text{For } v = 16, \quad c = 0.26.$$
$$\text{For } v = 64, \quad c = 0.13.$$
$$\text{For } v = 256, \quad c = 0.065.$$

A glance at these figures will show that a real constant would be obtained, if the values of c were multiplied by the square root of v in each case; thus,

$$0.26 \times \sqrt{16} = 0.13 \times \sqrt{64} = 0.065 \times \sqrt{256}.$$

We must then substitute for v, in the

* *Ztschr. phys. Chem.*, xvii. 385. The above paragraph is quoted from Theory of Electrolytic Dissociation, pp. 147-148.

Ostwald expression, the square root of v, when it becomes:

$$\frac{a^2}{(1-a)\sqrt{v}} = \text{constant.}$$

Rudolphi applied his equation to between fifty and sixty strongly dissociated compounds, and the values found for c approached a constant. While marked deviations are not wanting, yet Rudolphi's expression applies as well to the strongly dissociated electrolytes, as that of Ostwald to those which are less strongly dissociated, as the organic acids and bases. This will be seen from the following examples:

Hydrochloric Acid.		Potassium Sulphite.		Potassium Acetate.	
v	c	v	c	v	c
2	4.86	2	0.453	2	1.24
4	4.45	8	0.454	100	1.19
8	5.13	32	0.455	1,000	1.18
16	5.13	128	0.544	10,000	1.08

The Rudolphi expression is, of course, purely empirical. The physical significance of the $\sqrt{v}$ is thus far entirely unexplained. One or two modifications of the Rudolphi formula have been proposed, but these are also empirical, and cannot be regarded as essentially in advance of the original."

We have then, one dilution law holding for the weakly dissociated electrolytes, and another applying to the strongly dissociated compounds. The dilution law of Ostwald, which applies to the weakly dissociated compounds, has a rational basis, as we have seen; being deduced from an equation for a dissociating vapor, which was established not only empirically by direct experiment, but which has also been deduced thermodynamically. The physical significance of this law is perfectly apparent, but not so with the dilution law of Rudolphi, which applies to the strongly dissociated compounds. It has been established only by experiment, and is, therefore, purely empirical. Its rela-

tions to other things are not known, we have no idea what is the physical significance of the square root of v in expression. It, however, seems to fit facts in the cases of strongly dissociu substances, and we may some day learn significance.

These dilution laws are not simply wide-reaching generalizations, which embrace a large number of facts; as important as such generalizations always but they have a special significance. numerical values of the constants for ferent substances give us a world of formation about these compounds. *chemical activities of compounds are portional to these constants.* The significance of this relation may not pear at first sight. Its importance become apparent from the following considerations. By the chemical activity a substance we mean its power to en into chemical combinations with ot substances, how it will behave in the p ence of other compounds, what reacti it will effect, and the velocities with wl such reactions will take place; in a wo the entire chemical nature and conduct a substance. All this is given at once the value of the "Dissociation Consta of the substance, obtained from the d tion laws which we have just been c sidering. From such facts we can see real significance and importance of dilution laws, as expressing the relat between the dilution of the solution the dissociation of the dissolved substa

THE IONIZING POWER OF HEAT.

We have dealt thus far with electro dissociation as taking place only in s tions of certain substances in certain vents. A question which has thus far b unanswered is, what effect does rise in te perature have on the amount of the electrolyte which is dissociated? This question is made all the more prominent by the well-known fact that heat dissociates the vapors of many compounds like ammonium chloride, phosphorus pentachloride, etc.; and we have just pointed out a relation (Ostwald dilution law) between this dissociation into molecules by heat, and electrolytic dissociation into ions by solvents like water.

An investigation on the effect of temperature on electrolytic dissociation in aqueous solutions has been carried out in this laboratory* during the past year, and the result has been to show that between 0 degree and 35 degrees—the limits of the investigation—temperature has little or no effect on dissociation in solution.

We might conclude from the above fact that heat has no power to break molecules down into ions, but such a conclusion would not be justified. We must first study the effect of heat alone, when there is no solvent present. To do this we must heat the dry compound, perhaps to its fusion point, to see whether in fused electrolytes there is any evidence of the presence of ions. The result can be stated in a word. Many electrolytes when fused, conduct the current to a very considerable extent. Some of the compounds thus far studied are sodium and calcium chlorides, potassium bromide and iodide, potassium, ammonium, and silver nitrates, etc. The evidence is perfectly clear that heat, as well as solvents, can ionize molecules; i. e., can effect electrolytic dissociation.

WAYS IN WHICH IONS ARE FORMED.

This rather long chapter will be con-

---

*Results will soon appear in *American Chemical Journal*.

cluded with some account of the different ways in which ions are formed from molecules. The conclusion to which one would be led at first, from a general study of the whole subject, is that ions are formed from molecules in only one way— *a molecule, under certain conditions, breaking down into an equivalent number of cations and anions.* While this is the method most frequently met with in electrolytic dissociation, it is by no means the only method. That this method may be more clearly understood, and for the sake of comparison with other methods, a few examples of dissociation by this method are given:

$$HCl = \overset{+}{H} + \overset{-}{Cl} \qquad NaOH = \overset{+}{Na} + \overset{-}{OH}$$
$$HNO_3 = \overset{+}{H} + \overset{-}{NO_3} \qquad NH_4OH = \overset{+}{NH_4} + \overset{-}{OH}$$
$$H_2SO_4 = \overset{+}{H} + \overset{-}{HSO_4} \qquad Ba(OH)_2 = \overset{++}{Ba} + \overset{-}{OH} + \overset{-}{OH}$$
$$\overset{-}{HSO_4} = \overset{+}{H} + \overset{=}{SO_4}$$

$$KCl = \overset{+}{K} + \overset{-}{Cl}$$
$$K_2SO_4 = \overset{+}{K} + \overset{+}{K} + \overset{=}{SO_4}$$
$$BaCl_2 = \overset{++}{Ba} + \overset{-}{Cl} + \overset{-}{Cl}$$
$$CuSO_4 = \overset{++}{Cu} + \overset{=}{SO_4}$$

These examples of acids, bases, and salts, suffice to illustrate the principle, which is exemplified whenever these compounds dissolve in a strongly dissociating solvent like water.

Another entirely different method of ion formation is exemplified when *an atom takes a charge from an ion, becoming itself an ion, the original ion becoming an atom.* This takes place when a metal like zinc is brought in contact with a solution of a salt of another metal like copper. The copper which is in the ionic state gives up its charge to the zinc, becoming itself an atom, while the zinc atom, having taken the charge from the copper, becomes an ion. This mode of ion formation would be expressed thus:

$$\overset{++}{Cu} + \overset{=}{SO_4} + Zn = \overset{++}{Zn} + \overset{=}{SO_4} + Cu.$$

There is no change whatever in the anion. It remains in the solution after the reaction, in exactly the same condition as before. The copper ion gives up its charge to the zinc and is precipitated as metallic copper. This mode of ion formation explains all those chemical reactions in which one metal precipitates another metal from its salts. All that takes place in such reactions is the transfer of the electrical charge from the metal which is precipitated, to the metal which passes into solution in the ionic state.

A third mode of ion formation differs fundamentally from the two modes just considered: *One substance passes from the atom into a cation, another substance at the same time passing from the atom into the corresponding anion.* The example of this mode of ion formation which is usually cited, is the solution of gold in chlorine water. Metallic gold in the presence of water does not form ions to any appreciable extent, and chlorine in the presence of water does not form ions to any appreciable extent. If metallic gold and ordinary chlorine are brought into the presence of water simultaneously, the gold passes over to the cationic condition, and the chlorine forms an equivalent number of anions, in the sense of the following equation:

$$Au + Cl + Cl + Cl = \overset{+++}{Au} + \overset{-}{Cl} + \overset{-}{Cl} + \overset{-}{Cl}.$$

We have thus an insight into the mechanism of what takes place in a reaction which was hitherto simply described as the "solution of gold in chlorine water," which was, of course, simply renaming the phenomena. This is another of the many examples of the way in which the theory of electrolytic dissociation has thrown light on chemical problems. We may look upon the reaction thus: The neutral gold takes positive electricity from the neutral chlorine, becoming positively charged, while the chlorine having lost positive electricity is no longer electrically neutral, but becomes negatively charged.

The fourth and last mode of ion formation is in a certain sense the most important, in that it deals with many of the phenomena in chemistry which are referred to as oxidation and reduction. *An ion takes on an additional charge of electricity, converting an atom into an ion with the opposite charge.* This is very simply illustrated by the case of ferrous chloride and chlorine. Ferrous chloride in the presence of chlorine becomes ferric chloride, in the sense of the following equation:

$$\overset{++}{Fe} + \overset{-}{Cl} + \overset{-}{Cl} + Cl = \overset{+++}{Fe} + \overset{-}{Cl} + \overset{-}{Cl} + \overset{-}{Cl}.$$

The ferrous ion with its two charges takes up a third charge and becomes a ferric ion, at the same time converting a chlorine atom into a chlorine ion. This will be recognized at once as an example of what in chemistry is known as oxidation. The terms oxidation and reduction in chemistry are used in two senses. They mean the addition of oxygen or the addition of hydrogen. They are also used in an entirely different sense, as meaning the increase or decrease of the valence of a substance; and since we now deal with valence in terms of Faraday's law, and mean by it the number of charges upon the ions, oxidation means simply the increase in the number of charges upon the ion, and reduction a decrease in this number.

Using oxidation in this latter sense we see that the above mode of ion formation is an example of it; ferrous iron with two positive charges passing into ferric iron with three positive charges. Reduction is, of course, exactly the reverse process; *i. e.*, the removal of some of the charges already present upon the ion.

We have, then, in this mode of ion formation, a physical explanation of what takes place in oxidation and reduction reactions, when these terms are used in the second of the two senses referred to above.

The above four include all the modes by which ions are formed from molecules. If we study them carefully in their bearing on chemical reactions in general, we shall see that they furnish a physical basis for a large number of reactions, whose meaning was hitherto entirely concealed.

In the light of what has thus far been brought out in these papers, we should begin to see the importance of the theory of electrolytic dissociation as applied to chemical phenomena. In the following chapter the bearing of this and other generalizations on a strictly electrochemical problem will be pointed out.

CHAPTER VII—CALCULATION OF THE ELECT
MOTIVE FORCE OF ELEMENTS.

PART I.

IN the six preceding chapters we have traced the development of the fundamental conceptions which underlie modern electrochemistry. In the first chapter we studied osmotic pressure, and showed how the relations between gas-pressure and osmotic pressure were discovered. The origin of the theory of electrolytic dissociation was traced in the second chapter, together with some lines of evidence bearing upon it. In the third, certain applications of this theory were taken up. The fourth was devoted to electrolysis and the decomposition of electrolytes in general, by the current; the theories to account for electrolysis receiving special attention. Chapter five was devoted to the determination of the relative and absolute velocities of ions, and chapter six discussed the conductivity of electrolytes, and especially the application of the conductivity method to the measurement of electrolytic dissociation.

These chapters have, in a sense, been preliminary to the one which is to follow. We shall aim to show in this chapter how these fundamental conceptions have been applied to a problem of both scientific and technical importance—the calculation of the electromotive force of elements. This problem is interesting scientifically, because, for the first time, we are able to obtain any adequate conception of what takes place in a primary battery, and although such batteries have been known for more than a century, their action has been explained for only about a dozen years.

The problem is of technical inte cause it enables the engineer to de primary cells in a theoretical r which is as simple mathematically can ever hope such a problem to

We can, of course, assume th methods of measuring the electr force of elements are familiar to shall proceed at once to the applica the conceptions developed in these to the problem in hand.

It should be stated at the outset nature of the problem is not a simp The primary cell in its simplest a complicated device, involving a of processes and operations; and th of the action of these cells involv essarily, a number of conceptions must be clearly grasped before the ing deductions can be appreciated. these conceptions have already beer oped at sufficient length, but one additional features must be introd the proper places. Because a prol a little complex, however, should barrier to its solution, but, on th trary, should be an incentive to effort. It is believed that the fi solution will offer no serious diffic any one who has followed the pr chapters, and who has even an elen knowledge of the calculus.

CALCULATION OF THE ELECTR
FORCE OF ELEMENTS FROM T
MOTIC PRESSURES OF THE SOL
AROUND THE ELECTRODES.

The first time that one comes up heading it is safe to predict that its

ing will not be fully understood. How is it possible to calculate the electromotive force of primary cells, from the osmotic pressure of the electrolytes around the poles? How could there be any close connection between osmotic pressure and the potential in a cell?—are questions which are almost sure to be asked at the outset. Indeed, it is difficult to see off-hand that there is any connection between two sets of phenomena apparently so widely removed from one another.

A careful study of these phenomena will bring out the fact that there is a very close relation, indeed, between them; as so frequently manifests itself, when we come to consider apparently disconnected phenomena in the light of some recently discovered generalization.

It should be stated at the outset that the very important deductions which are to be followed in this chapter we owe almost entirely to Nernst, who worked them out theoretically and verified many of them experimentally, while a privat-docent in the laboratory of Ostwald, in Leipzig.*

The fundamental principle which makes the following deduction possible, is that if we allow a substance under one condition to pass into another condition, isothermally, it makes no difference how the transformation takes place; *i. e.*, whether we allow it to be accomplished osmotically by the flow of the solvent from one solution to another, or electrically, by the flow of a current and the consequent movement of the ions.

We must first find out the *maximum amount of external work* which can be obtained from a process, in which a substance passes isothermally from one condition over to another. This can be most readily accomplished by starting with a gas under one pressure, and allowing it to expand, isothermally, until it is under a considerably smaller pressure; since, as already stated in these papers, we know more about matter in the gaseous than in any other condition, and can deal with it far more freely.

Let us start with the gas under any pressure p_1 and volume v_1, and allow it to expand isothermally until it is under a considerably smaller pressure, which we will call p_2, to distinguish it from the first pressure which the gas exerted. When a gas expands thus, isothermally, it does work as we say, in overcoming the pressure of the atmosphere; or, to use technical terms, it takes up heat from the surrounding objects and converts it into energy of volume, which it can again give up. The amount of this is, from the well-known thermodynamic principle:

$$-\int_{p_1}^{p_2} v\,dp \dots\dots\dots\dots(1)$$

If we represent the pressure of a gas by p_1 and its volume by v_1, the combined expression of the laws of Boyle and Gay Lussac is; $pv = \mathrm{RT}$, where R is the well-known gas constant and T the absolute temperature of the gas.

Substituting $pv = \mathrm{RT}$ in equation (1) we have:

$$\mathrm{RT}\int_{p_1}^{p_2} \frac{dp}{p} \dots\dots\dots\dots(2)$$

an expression for the volume energy obtainable from an expanding gas, which can be readily integrated.

* For a fuller discussion of this whole subject, see ....'s Lehrbuch der Allgemeinen Chemie, Le Blanc's ...., or Jones's Theory of Electrolytic Disso-

The integral is :

$$RT \ln \frac{p_1}{p_2} \quad \ldots \ldots \ldots \ldots (3)$$

which is an expression of the amount of energy converted into work, which can be obtained from a gas obeying the gas laws, expanding isothermally from any pressure p_1 to any other pressure p_2.

The question which arises here is what connection exists between the above deduction for a gas and the osmotic pressure of a solution? What has the one to do with the other? We will recall in this connection the contents of the first chapter, where it was shown that the osmotic pressure of solutions obeys the gas-laws, and we can see now one of the many applications of this highly important generalization.

Since the laws of gas-pressure apply to the osmotic pressure of solutions, we can apply any deduction from the one set of phenomena directly to the other set. The work obtainable from an ideal gas, in passing from a gas-pressure p_1 to a gas-pressure p_2 is, therefore, exactly equal to that which can be obtained from an ideal solution in passing from an osmotic pressure p_1 to an osmotic pressure p_2. In the above deduction the gas had a volume v, and passed isothermally from the one pressure over to the other. In order that the conditions should be comparable for the solution, it must also have a volume* v, and pass isothermally from the one pressure over to the other.

The all important point in the calculation of the electromotive force of elements from osmotic pressure, is the following : *The ions cannot move in a solution without carrying with them the electrical*

charges *which are upon them,* (*amount of work obtainable from* (*in passing from one osmotic pres* *another, can be transformed in* *trical energy.* This is the key to th deduction which follows. We h ready seen how to calculate the .w tainable from an isothermal tran tion of ions from one osmotic 1 to another. Since this work can b formed into electrical energy, equate the maximum external wor. is obtainable and the electrical which is equal to it.

We have thus far shown how culate the electrical energy ob: from a solution whose ions are u osmotic pressure p_1, in passing osmotic pressure p_2. But electrical is one thing, and potential or electr force is another. This brings the second important step, *what* (*exists between electrical energy* (*tential?*

Electrical energy, like every othe festation of energy, can be rega: made up of two factors; the one ex the quantity of energy and the ot intensity of the energy. In brief, ' a *capacity* and an *intensity* factor, product of these two is, of cours to the energy in question.

In the case of electrical ene: *intensity factor is the potential,* (*capacity factor is the quantity* (*tricity.* The product of these two : to the electrical energy. If we re the electrical energy by E_e, as is done, the quantity of electricity by the potential by π, we have :

$$\pi E_0 = E_e \quad \ldots \ldots \ldots$$

We know E_e. since it is equal to tl imum external work obtainable fr

---

* By volume of a solution is meant the number of litres which contains a gram molecular weight of the electrolyte

isothermal transformation discussed above, we know E_0 or the quantity of electricity carried by a given quantity of ions in passing from one osmotic pressure over to another; since from Faraday's law this is determined once for all for any given ion, and knowing the quantity for any given univalent ion, we obtain it for an ion of any valence by simply multiplying this quantity by the valence of the ion in question. From equation 4, we have,

$$\pi = \frac{E_e}{E_0}$$

"Let* us deal with a gram-molecular weight of univalent ions. These will carry 96,540 coulombs of electricity, and this quantity we will now designate by E_0. If the ions are bivalent they will carry twice as much; if trivalent three times as much, and so on. Let us represent the valence of the ions by v; then, a gram-molecular weight will carry $v\,E_0$ of electricity. Suppose a gram-molecular weight of these ions are charged π potential. The amount of electrical energy required to effect this charge is:

$$\pi\,v\,E_0.$$

But this electrical energy is equal to the osmotic, calculated above, where a gram-molecular weight was taken into account. We have:

$$\pi\,v\,E_0 = -\,RT \ln \frac{p_1}{p_2} \ \text{or,}$$

$$\pi = -\,\frac{RT \ln \dfrac{p'}{p^2}}{v\,E_0} \ldots\ldots\ldots (5)$$

This is the fundamental equation for calculating the electromotive force of

* This paragraph is quoted from Theory of Electrolytic Dissociation, by Jones, pp. 229-230.

elements, from the osmotic pressures of the electrolytes around the electrodes."

Numerical values for a number of the quantities in the above equation are known, and can be readily inserted into it. Thus T, the absolute temperature of an ordinary room, can be taken as about 290 degrees (273 + 17). If we are dealing with gram-molecular weights of substances, R the gas-constant is two calories, or near enough to it for all practical purposes; and one calorie is equal to $4.18 + 10^7$ ergs. E_0, the quantity of electricity carried by a gram-molecular weight of univalent ions, is 96,540 coulombs. We have, then,

$$\frac{RT}{E_0} = 0.0251 \text{ volt,}$$

since a volt multiplied by a coulomb is equal to 10^7 ergs.

Substituting this value in equation 5, we would have:

$$\pi = \frac{0.0251}{v} \ln \frac{p_1}{p_2} \qquad (6)$$

If we wish to pass from the natural to the Briggsian logarithm, we must divide by 0.4343, when the above expression becomes:

$$\pi = \frac{0.058}{v} \log \frac{p_1}{p_2} \qquad (7)$$

If we are dealing with univalent ions, $v = 1$, when we have:

$$\pi = 0.058 \log \frac{p_1}{p_2} \qquad (8)$$

This is the form in which we shall use the equation in all calculations of the electromotive force of elements.

This equation takes into account nothing but the osmotic pressures of the ions in the solutions around the electrodes. It contains no factor which says anything about the nature of the electrodes used, or of any relation between the electrodes and the electrolytes in which they are immersed. The story of the action of the cell, as thus far told, is very important, but it is not the whole story. It is self-evident from our knowledge of primary cells that the electrodes as well as the electrolytes must be taken into account, and we shall now see the way in which this is done. This second important deduction, like the one which we have just considered, we owe to Nernst, who was the first to explain the action of the primary cell.

THE SOLUTION-TENSION OF METALS.

The term solution-tension of metals is now so extensively used, that every one must have some conception as to what is meant by it. From this, the term solution-tension has extended to every substance which dissolves in any solvent, so that solution-tension has become coextensive with the term solution itself. While a general conception is held as to what is meant by solution-tension, the exact use of the term must be understood before it can be used in connection with the electromotive force of elements. By solution-tension of metals we should understand that tension or strain analogous to a force, which tends to drive the atoms of metals off into the surrounding solvent. When the atoms are driven into solution, they are no longer present as atoms, but become ions. To illustrate: whenever a bar of metal is immersed in water, a few of the metallic atoms pass into the solution as ions; or, as we say, the metal dissolves to a slight extent. The number of metallic ions sent into the solution is very small in any case, and in most cases so small that they cannot be detected by or-

dinary chemical methods, yet we good theoretic ground for believing every metal dissolves in every solven slight extent—even platinum dissol water to an infinitesimal extent.

Nernst, who proposed this idea solution-tension of metals, driving metallic ions into the solvent, sugg that it was analogous to the vapor-te of liquids, which drives the liquid cules into the space above the liquid, for a given temperature, a definite pressure is reached.· When this press attained, the vapor-tension—still con ing to manifest itself—drives mol into space, but the number of mol which condense in a given time is equal to the number which evapo This is the condition known as eq rium.

The solution-tension acts in an gous manner, driving ions into so until a certain concentration is rea when just as many ions separate fro solution on to the bar of metal, in a time, as pass into solution. In the of Nernst:* "If, in accordance with Hoff's theory, we assume that the oules of a substance in solution exis under a definite pressure, we must a to a dissolving substance in contact a solvent, similarly, a power of expa for here also the molecules are drive a space in which they exist under a c pressure. It is evident that every stance will pass into solution, unt osmotic partial pressure of the mol in the solution is equal to the sol tension of the substance."

Nernst stated the whole subject o tion-tension of metals so clearly in hi inal, epoch-making paper, in which tl

---

* Ztschr. phys. Chem., iv, 180.

tents of this chapter were discussed, that we cannot do better than give his own words as literally as possible; since, from the importance of the subject dealt with, they have become of historical value:

"Let[*] us now consider what will take place if we dip a metal whose electrolytic solution-tension is P into a solution of one of its salts; the osmotic pressure of the metal ions in this solution being p. Let at first $P > p$; at the moment of contact a number of positively charged metallic ions, driven by this larger pressure, will pass into solution. Since by the latter a certain amount of positive electricity is carried from the metal into the solution, the liquid receives a positive charge, which arranges itself in the form of the positive ions contained in the solution, on the surface of the metal. At the same time there is, of course, a corresponding amount of negative electricity set free in the metal, which also passes to the surface of the metal. We recognize at once, that at the surface of contact of metal and electrolyte the two kinds of electricity must accumulate in the form of a double layer, whose existence, as is well known, was made probable some time ago by Von Helmholtz, in an entirely different way.

"This double layer furnishes one component of force, which acts at right angles to the surface of contact of the metal and the electrolyte, and which tends to drive the metallic ions from the electrolyte on to the metal, and thus acts in opposition to the solution-tension. Equilibrium will be, of course, established when these two forces equalize one another. The final result will be the appearance of an electromotive force between the metal and the electrolyte, which will give rise to a gal-

vanio current from the metal to the liquid, if by any device its existence is made possible.

"If $P < p$ the reverse of course takes place. Metallic ions separate from the electrolyte and are precipitated on to the metal, until the electrostatic component of force of the positive charge of the metal and the negative charge of the liquid, thus produced, are in equilibrium with the excess of osmotic pressure. An electromotive force again appears between the metal and the electrolyte, which, under suitable conditions, gives rise to a galvanic current, but in this case opposite in direction to the case first considered.

"If, finally, $P = p$, the metal and electrolyte are in equilibrium at the first moment of contact; therefore, no difference in potential exists between the two."

This clear and concise statement needs no comment and but little elaboration. If the solution-tension of the metal is greater than the osmotic pressure of the metallic ions in the solution, the action of the double layer is to oppose the greater pressure, which, in this case, is the solution-tension of the metal. If, on the other hand, the osmotic pressure of the metal ions in solution is greater than the solution-tension of the metal, a double layer is formed in such a sense as to oppose again the greater pressure, but in this case the greater pressure is the osmotic pressure.

In the first case the action of the double layer is, therefore, to drive metallic ions out of the solution on to the metal, in opposition to the solution-tension; in the second case the double layer tends to drive ions off from the metal into the solution, in opposition to the osmotic pressure of the ions already in solution.

---

[*] Ztschr. phys. Chem., iv, 151-152.

The action of the double layer in both cases is to establish equilibrium between the solution-tension of the metal and the osmotic pressure of the metal ions in solution, and to do this it must, of course, always act against the greater force.

"If,[*] now, we inquire which metals have high and which low solution-tensions, we will find that magnesium, zinc, aluminum, cadmium, iron, cobalt, nickel, and the like, are always negative when immersed in solutions of their own salts. This means that the solution-tension of the metal is always greater than the osmotic pressure of the metal ion, in any solution of their salts which can be prepared. If, on the other hand, we take gold, silver, mercury, copper, etc., we usually find the metal positive when immersed in a solution of its salt. This means that the solution-tension of the metal is so small, that it is less than the osmotic pressure of the metallic ion in the solution. When a very dilute solution of salts of these metals is prepared, the osmotic pressure of the metallic ion may become less than the very slight solution-tension of these metals, and then the metal would be negative with respect to its solution."

A DEMONSTRATION OF THE SOLUTION-TEN-
SION OF METALS.

One might easily think that this conception of the solution-tension of metals is all very well, as a matter of pure theory, and may, perhaps, help us in our explanation of the action of primary cells, but the most important question is, what evidence have we that it is true? Indeed, there has been absolutely no evidence presented thus far; and does it not,

[*] Quoted from Theory of Electrolytic Dissociation, p. 285.

after all, seem a little contradictory to experience? If metals all dissolve water and similar solvents, as this ception demands, why do they not solve in quantities sufficient to be dete by our most refined chemical meth

This is a very natural state of mind one to be in with respect to the w problem, until the evidence for this is presented and carefully considered

With respect to the point raised a that if metals like gold, platinum, si etc., dissolve in water, they dissolv such small quantity that it canno detected, it need only be recalled that ions carry enormous quantities of tricity. A gram-molecular weight univalent ions carries 96,540 coulo as we have already seen. The n ber of ions which would pass solution in order to establish a consi able difference in potential between metal and the solution, would be small indeed. It has been calculated the number required to produce the ferences in potential which actnally e would be far too small in the case such metals as those named above, to b tected by the most refined methods kn to man. This apparent discrepancy then, not at all at variance with the ception of the solution-tension of me but is exactly in accord with it, and e have been predicted beforehand with greatest certainty.

It is, however, one thing to remove jections to a theory or conception, an is quite a different matter to bring ward positive evidence of its truth. shall now consider a demonstration of solution-tension of metals, which seem leave little to be desired. The follo demonstration was furnished by maer: Mercury* is a metal whose solution-tension is very small. Even when in contact with a very dilute solution of a mercury salt, the solution-tension of the mercury is less than the osmotic pressure of the mercury ions in the solution, and some of the mercury ions will separate from such a solution. Given a vessel whose bottom is covered with metallic mercury, and over this is placed a solution of mercurous nitrate, having a volume of 2,000; a few mercury ions will separate from the solution and give up their positive charges to the mercury. The positively charged mercury will attract, electrostatically, a few negative $\overline{NO_3}$ ions to form the double layer. This will be continued until a certain difference in potential has been reached, when equilibrium will be established. If, now, a drop of mercury is let fall into the solution, a few mercury ions will separate upon it, charge it positively, and it will then attract an equal number of negative NO_3 ions, and drag them down with it through the solution. The next drop of mercury will behave in exactly the same manner, and thus the top of the solution will become continually poorer and poorer in salt.

When the drop of mercury comes in contact with the mercury at the bottom of the vessel, where equilibrium is already established, what will happen? When the drop has united with the mercury, this will contain an excess of positive electricity and, therefore, a small quantity of mercury ions will pass into solution; and, indeed, exactly the same number as there are $\overline{NO_3}$ ions carried down from

the top to the bottom of the solution. The solution will thus become more concentrated just above the layer of mercury on the bottom of the vessel.

A fine glass tube from which mercury flows is known as a drop-electrode. To produce changes in concentration sufficient for the purposes of a demonstration, a very powerful drop-electrode must be used. This is made by inserting a conical glass-stopper into a conical glass tube, so that the junction is mercury-tight. A large number of fine grooves are then etched on the outside of the stopper, so

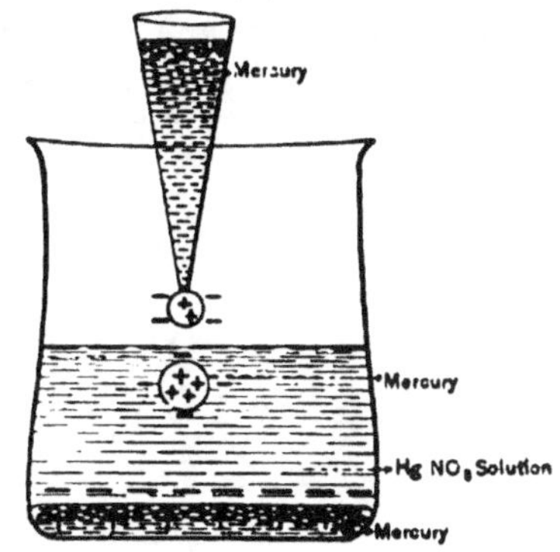

FIG. 10. APPARATUS TO ILLUSTRATE SOLUTION TENSION OF METALS.

that the mercury will stream through as a fine mist. To assist this process the mercury cannot be allowed to flow dipheres of pressure.

Under these conditions, however, the mercury can not be allowed to flow directly into a vessel filled with a dilute solution of a mercury salt, and containing mercury at the bottom, since there would be too much commotion in the solution. The arrangement which was used is shown in the accompanying sketch, Fig. 10.

---

* *Ztschr. phys. Chem.* xxv. 266; xxviii. 257. Also *Ztschr. elek. Chem.*, vii. 357. The above description is quoted from Elements of Physical Chemistry by H. C. Jones, which will soon be published by the Macmillans.

Here the mercury is allowed to flow directly into the solution, but the principle involved is exactly the same.

The drop-electrode dips into a funnel-shaped vessel, which is connected by a narrow tube and a rubber tube with a larger vessel. This is in turn connected with a vessel where the change in concentration can be observed. When the mercury has been allowed to flow for five minutes under a pressure of five atmospheres, distinct changes in concentration can be detected.

Palmaer gives data which show that the *concentration above had been diminished as much as fifty per cent, and increased below as much as forty per cent.*

This will be recognized at once to be a very remarkable experiment, and before the conception of solution-tension of metals was proposed, would have been entirely inexplicable. It should be added that the results of this experiment were all predicted before the experiment was tried.

We have developed in the first section of this chapter the method of calculating potential, or electromotive force, from the osmotic pressure of the solutions around the electrodes. Also the conception of the solution-tension of metals, and the way in which this acts when a metal is immersed in a solution of one of its salts. In the following section we shall apply these two fundamental conceptions to the electromotive force of primary cells.

CHAPTER VII—CALCULATION OF THE ELECTRO-MOTIVE FORCE OF ELEMENTS.

PART II.

THE CALCULATION OF THE DIFFERENCE IN POTENTIAL BETWEEN A METAL AND A SOLUTION OF ONE OF ITS SALTS.

We have already seen how it is possible to calculate potential from the osmotic pressure of the solutions around the electrodes, and have also studied the solution-tension of metals, and what takes place when a metal is immersed in a solution of one of its salts. We shall now apply these two fundamental conceptions to the calculation of the difference in potential between a metal and a solution of one of its salts in which it is immersed.

Let us take a metal with a solution-tension P, and dip it into a solution of one of its salts, in which the metal ions have an osmotic pressure p; a difference in potential between the metal and the solution will result, and this can be calculated as follows from the foregoing conceptions.

The metal has a solution-tension P; this can be converted into ions under an osmotic pressure P, without any work being done. If the osmotic pressure of the metal ions in the solution is p, to convert a metal of solution-tension P into ions of an osmotic pressure p requires the same amount of work, or the same amount of work is obtainable, as if we started with the metal in the form of ions under an osmotic pressure P, and transformed them to a condition where the osmotic pressure was p. Since the laws of gas-pressure apply to osmotic pressure, we can calculate the amount of work obtainable from the process where ions under an osmotic pressure P are transformed into ions under an osmotic pressure p, from a gas under a gas-pressure P when transformed to a gas-pressure p. In the first part of this chapter this was shown to be, for a gram-molecular weight of a gas,

$$\text{RT ln } \frac{P}{p}$$

We have also seen that this is equal to the electrical energy which can be obtained from such a process, since the work done is transformable, quantitatively, into electrical energy, when we are dealing with solutions under suitable conditions. The electrical energy E_e is equal to the potential π, times the capacity E_0—

$$E_e = \pi E_0$$

If then we equate these two equal values we have:

$$\pi E_0 = \text{RT ln } \frac{P}{p}$$

If now we introduce the numerical values already given for $\dfrac{RT}{E_0}$, and solve for π, at the same time changing to Briggsian logarithm, we would have:

$$\pi = 0.058 \log \frac{P}{p}$$

The difference between the potential of a metal and a solution of one of its salts in which it is immersed is, then, equal to a constant, which, for 290 degrees absolute temperature, or the temperature of the ordinary room, is 0.058 volt, into the logarithm of the solution-tension of the metal, minus the logarithm of the osmotic pressure of the metal ions in the solution. We shall now apply the conceptions with which we have become familiar to a few typical elements.

TYPES OF ELEMENTS.

We know a large number of primary cells, and these are constructed of very different substances for the electrodes, and of solutions of very different electrolytes. In all such cells it should be observed that we have both classes of conductors; those of the first class conducting like the metals and serving as the electrodes, and surrounding these are conductors of the second class or solutions of some electrolyte or electrolytes. To construct a primary battery it is then necessary to have conductors of the first class in contact with conductors of the second class.

A system of classification has been adopted for primary cells, which simplifies the whole class very greatly. If during the action of the cell its electromotive force does not change, it is called a *constant* element. If it does, the element is *inconstant*. In order that the electromotive force of an element should remain constant, it is necessary that the process which goes on in the cell should remain unchanged as long as the cell is in action.

Through some constant elements a current can be passed in a direction the opposite to that in which the current would normally flow, without changing the electromotive force of the element. Such constant elements are known as *reversible*. In order that an element should be reversible it is necessary that the reverse current should not change the nature of the element. This can only happen when the electrodes are immersed in solutions of their own salts. In such cases the reverse current simply causes a deposition of

a small amount of one metal, and the solution of a corresponding amount of the other. When the reverse current is passed for a very short time the nature of the element remains essentially unaltered. There are other constant elements through which a current cannot be sent in the reverse direction without changing the nature of the element and, consequently, its electromotive force. Such constant elements are termed *irreversible*.

We shall take up first a very simple, reversible, constant element, and apply the conceptions already developed to the calculation of its electromotive force.

A SIMPLE CONCENTRATION ELEMENT.

The simplest primary cell of which we can conceive, consists of one electrolyte of two different concentrations, and one electrode. Into a beaker pour a concentrated solution of stannous chloride until it is about half full. Immerse a bar of tin into the solution, of such a length that it is about half covered with the concentrated solution of the salt. Then pour carefully on to this concentrated solution a dilute solution of the same salt, until the beaker is nearly filled.

Let us now see what takes place in the above arrangement. Where the tin is surrounded by the more concentrated solution of stannous chloride, it increases in size, due to the separation of the metal from the solution on to the bar. The ions of tin, when they separate in the metallic condition, give up their charges to this portion of the bar, which becomes charged strongly positive. This charge flows along the whole bar, since the metal is a good conductor, and the entire bar of tin becomes charged positively by just so much as there are ions separated as metal on to the bar. If this charge could not escape in some way, the difference between the potential of the bar and that of the solution (which has become negative due to the loss of positive ions) would very quickly become so great, that no further separation of ions in the form of metal on to the bar would be possible. The original action would very quickly cease, were it not for the fact that the bar, when charged positively, is just in the condition most favorable to giving off ions to the more dilute solution of stannous chloride, and it does so. When a metal passes into solution as ions it must obtain positive electricity from some source. In this case the positive electricity is already present on the bar, the atoms take it up, become ions, and pass into the solution. This lowers the potential of the bar again, and more ions can separate from the solution; and the process is, thus, a continuous one.

The action of this, the simplest of all primary elements, is as follows: Tin ions separate from the more concentrated solution of stannous chloride, on to that portion of the bar immersed in this solution. They give up their charges to this portion of the bar, which are then conducted to the portion immersed in the more dilute solution. Here atoms of tin take up the positive electricity, become ions, and pass into solution. The chlorine ions have, meanwhile, traveled from the more concentrated toward the more diluted solution, against the direction of flow of the current.

The action of this cell, like the action of all concentration elements, is such as to decrease the concentration of the more concentrated solution, and to increase the concentration of the more dilute solution. This would continue until the concentrations of the two solutions would become

the same, when the element would cease to be an element.

It would be extremely difficult to measure the electromotive force of such an element as that just described, and it would, therefore, be of little value to calculate it, since it could not be verified by experiment. We will, then, use this element as an illustration of the very simplest concentration element, and proceed to apply our deductions to a concentration element whose electromotive force can be measured.

The element which we shall study, both theoretically and practically, consists of two bars of zinc, immersed, the one in a more concentrated solution of zinc chloride, and the other in a more diluted solution of the same electrolyte. The arrangement would be illustrated by the following sketch.

Two bars of zinc serve as the electrodes, and are connected with a strip of zinc. These dip into solutions of zinc chloride of different concentrations. The concentrations are represented for convenience as one-tenth and one-hundredth normal. The two solutions are connected by means of a siphon, filled either with the tenth or with the hundredth-normal solution. The ends of the siphon are filled with loose rolls of filter paper, to prevent a mechanical mixing of the solutions, and to lessen the rate at which one solution will diffuse over into the other. The filter paper offers a comparatively slight resistance to the passage of the current.

It will be observed that both electrodes are of the same metal, and that they are immersed in solutions of the same electrolyte; the only difference on the two sides of the cell being that the solutions of the zinc chloride are of different concentrations.

Hence the name, *concentration element*.

The action of this element will be very readily understood from the explanation of the action of the simpler concentration element, consisting of one bar of tin immersed in two solutions of stannous chloride. Take first the side of the element on which the electrolyte is more concentrated. Zinc is an element, as we shall see, which has a very high solution-tension. This is always much greater than the osmotic pressure of even the most concentrated solutions of zinc chloride which can be prepared. When a bar of zinc is immersed in any solution of zinc chloride,

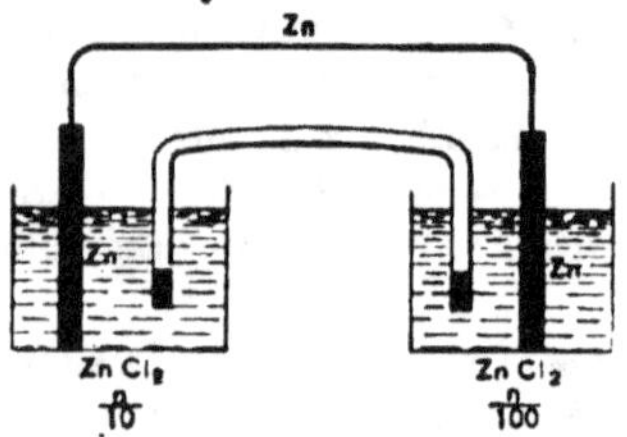

FIG. 11. CONCENTRATION ELEMENT.

it always sends off some ions into the solution, and establishes the double layer in the sense to oppose the further ionization and solution of the zinc. The zinc bar then becomes negative and the solution positive. Suppose at first that the circuit is not closed, this will take place on both sides of the cell, until equilibrium is established between the solution-tension of the zinc and the electrical double layer formed. It will, however, be remembered, that when the solution-tension of the metal P is greater than the osmotic pressure of the metal ions p, $(P > p)$ the double layer will be formed so as to assist the osmotic pressure or the smaller value, in overcoming the larger value or the solution-tension. In such cases equilibrium will be reached when the sum of the osmotic pressure of the metal ions, and the action of the double layer, are just equal to the solution-tension of the metal. Therefore, the larger the osmotic pressure, the smaller the action of the double layer which will be necessary to equalize the solution-tension.

The osmotic pressure of the zinc ions is, of course, larger on the side of the cell containing the more concentrated solution,* and, consequently, the action of the double layer will be less on this side of the cell. But the action of the double layer depends on the difference in potential between the metal and the solution, and this depends upon the number of zinc ions which pass into solution. On the side of the cell containing the more concentrated solution, the zinc will send fewer ions into the solution than on the opposite side, and, consequently, its potential will not be as much reduced as on the other side. The bar of zinc in the more concentrated solution, like the bar in the more dilute, will become negative, but not as much negative as the bar in the more dilute solution.

Suppose, now, the two sides of the cell are connected, what will happen? The bar in the more concentrated solution is less negative than the bar in the more dilute; consequently, when the two are connected a current will flow from the former to the latter, or the former will be the positive pole. Upon this pole, when the circuit is closed, zinc will be deposited. The zinc ions give up their charges to it and separate in the metallic condition, and, consequently, this becomes the cathode. On the other side of the

---

* A word of explanation here may almost seem superfluous; but the error is frequently made of regarding a more dilute solution as containing the larger number of ions, because the percentage of dissociation is larger in the dilute solution.

cell zinc atoms are taking up positive charges, becoming zinc ions, which separate from the bar and pass into solution. This bar, having lost negative electricity, becomes the negative pole or the anode. The action of the cell is, then, to decrease the number of zinc ions on the more concentrated side, and to increase the number on the more dilute side; the current flowing on the outside from the pole immersed in the more concentrated solution to the pole immersed in the more dilute. On the inside the current flows in the opposite direction, from the pole immersed in the more dilute solution; and, since the anions move against the current, the chlorine ions move over toward the pole immersed in the more dilute solution of zinc chloride. The more dilute solution thus becomes continually more concentrated, and the more concentrated more dilute. So much by way of explanation of what takes place. Let us now apply the conceptions and deductions with which we have been dealing in this type of concentration elements. The potential on the more concentrated side, between the metal and the electrolyte would be expressed thus:

$$\pi_1 = \frac{0.058}{v} \log \frac{P}{p_2}$$

where v is the valence of the zinc ion $= 2$, P the solution-tension of zinc, and p_2 the osmotic pressure of the zinc ions in the solution. The potential on the other side is:

$$\pi_2 = \frac{0.058}{v} \log \frac{P}{p_1}$$

where the common symbols have the same significance, and p_1 is the osmotic pressure of the zinc ions in the more dilute solution.

The electromotive force of this, as well as any other primary cell, is the difference between the potentials on the two sides, therefore:

$$\pi = \frac{0.058}{v} \log \frac{P}{p_2} - \frac{0.058}{v} \log \frac{P}{p_1}$$

$$= \frac{0.058}{v} \log \frac{p_1}{p_2}; \text{ and since } v = 2$$

$$\pi = 0.029 \log \frac{p_1}{p_2}$$

The metal being the same on both sides of the cell has the same solution-tension* on the two sides, and being of equal value and opposite sign disappears from the final equation.

From anything which has been said thus far, we might conclude that this was the entire story of the concentration element. There is, however, still one factor which has not been taken into account— the change in the concentration of the solutions which is taking place while the current is passing, due to the movement of the ions.†

"If E_0 electricity passes from the electrode into the electrolyte, a gram-molecular weight of univalent cations separates from the electrode, dissolves, and increases by unity the concentration around this electrode. But, at the same time, cations are moving from this electrode, with the current, over toward the other electrode. The amount depends upon the relative velocities of anion and cation. If we represent the relative velocity of cation by c, and of anion by a, the number of the cations which will move over with the current is $\frac{c}{c+a}$. The increase in the con-

---

centration, due to a gram-molecular weight of cations passing into solution, is then:

$$1 - \frac{c}{c + a} = \frac{a}{c + a}.$$

This factor is to be multiplied into the former equation to obtain the osmotic work, which can then be equated to its equal—the electrical energy. Let n_i represent the number of ions in a gram-molecular weight of the electrolyte:

$$\pi = \frac{a}{c + a} \; \frac{n_i \, RT}{v \, e_0} \ln \frac{p_1}{p_2};$$

or,

$$\pi = \frac{a}{c + a} \; \frac{n_i}{v} \; 0.058 \log \frac{p_1}{p_2} \text{''}$$

We have now taken into account all the factors involved in this simple concentration element. The osmotic pressures of the cations of the electrolyte, the solution-tension of the metal used as electrodes, and the velocities of the ions, have all been considered. The electromotive force of such an element depends, according to the final equation, chiefly upon the relative osmotic pressures of the cations of the electrolyte used ; but, in addition, upon the factor $\dfrac{a}{c + a}$, which must be taken into account for the reasons given above.

This equation has been applied to concentration elements analogous to the one just described, and their electromotive force calculated from the osmotic pressures of the electrolytes used, and the relative velocities of their ions. The electromotive forces of the same elements have then been measured, and the calculated values compared with those found experimentally. The two sets of values have been found to agree very satisfactorily in every case where a comparison has been made.

In an element such as has just been described, the only sources of potential are at the surfaces of contact of the electrodes with the electrolytes, and the surfaces of contact of the two electrolytes with each other. There is no source of potential at the contact of the two electrodes, since they are of the same metal. We should like to know how much of the electromotive force was generated at the contact of the metals with the electrolytes, and how much at the contacts of the two electrolytes.

The magnitude of the potential at the contact of the electrolytes can be calculated, and also measured, as Nernst has shown. To do this we must exclude the other source of potential, *viz.*, that at the contact of the electrodes with the electrolytes, and this has been done in a form of element which we shall now study.

THE LIQUID ELEMENT.

To determine the potential at the surface of contact of two electrolytes, the same metal must be used for electrodes on both sides of the cell, and both electrodes must dip into solutions of the same electrolyte, and of the same concentration. Such elements have been studied by Nernst,[*] who explained for the first time the action of the liquid element. As an example of the liquid element he cites the following:

$$\tfrac{n}{10}\,KCl - \tfrac{n}{100}\,KCl - \tfrac{n}{100}\,HCl - \tfrac{n}{10}\,HCl - \tfrac{n}{10}\,KCl$$

The platinum electrodes dip into the tenth-normal solutions of potassium chloride at the two ends, so that any potential generated here on one side, would be exactly balanced by the equal potential of opposite sign on the other side of the cell.

---

[*] *Ztschr. phys. Chem.*, iv, 140

The only sources of potential in such an element would be at the contacts of the solutions of the electrolytes.

The question which would naturally arise in connection with such an element is, why should there be any potential at all at the surface of contact of two electrolytes? Nernst thinks that this is due to the unequal velocities with which the ions move in a solution. The faster ion is held back in its movements by the slower, and the result is a tension which manifests itself as a potential. The words of Nernst in this connection will be given, introducing the symbols c and a for the relative velocities of cation and anion, respectively, instead of u and v which were employed by Nernst, and have since been generally used by those who have discussed these problems.

"Since* in electrolytes electricity can move only with the ponderable masses, the ions, we will find the difference in potential which exists between two solutions of the same electrolyte of different concentrations, which are in contact, by calculating the work required to transport the masses carrying the two kinds of electricity from the one solution to the other.

According to the views of Hittorf, and especially those developed later by Kohlrausch, the conductivity of a current of intensity i, in an electrolyte in which the cation has the velocity c, and the anion the velocity a, is always found as follows:

In unit time $i \dfrac{c}{c + a}$ of positive electricity

moves in the direction of the current,

and $i \dfrac{a}{c + a}$ of negative electricity moves in

the opposite direction. We have, therefore:

$$*\mathrm{E}' = \frac{c}{c + a}; \; \mathrm{E}'' = \frac{a}{c + a}$$

To calculate the work required to transport the positive ions combined with E′ from the more diluted to the more concentrated solution, and the negative ions combined with E″ from the more concentrated to the more dilute solution; let p_1 be the (osmotic) pressure of the anions and, of course, also of the cations, in the one solution, and p_2 in the other solution. In order to transport the positive electricity E′ from the one to the other solution, together with the ponderable masses combined with it from the pressure p_1 to the pressure p_2, and at the same time the ponderable masses combined with negative electricity E″ from the pressure p_2 to the pressure p_1, the following amounts of work would be required:

$$\frac{c}{c + a} \int_{p_1}^{p_2} v \, dp \; \text{ar.d} \; \frac{a}{c + a} \int_{p_2}^{p_1} v \, dp$$

where v is the volume occupied by the mass of the cation (or cations) combined with a plus unit or a minus unit of electricity. If for the purpose of integration we write the Mariotte-Boyle law in this form:

$$p v = p_0$$

where p_0 is the pressure in a solution which contains in unit volume unit plus electricity on the cations, and unit negative electricity on the anions. The sum of the two amounts of work is:

$$\mathrm{P}_1 - \mathrm{P}_2 = \frac{c - a}{c + a} \, p_0 \, \ln \frac{p_1}{p_2}$$

P_1 is the potential of the positive elec-

---

* *Zeschr. phys. Chem.*, iv, 186.

* E′ and E″ are the amounts, respectively, of positive and negative electricity.

tricity E', and P_2 the potential of the negative electricity E''."

The above words are given because of their importance in connection with the history of this subject. They explain the action of the element in hand for the first time, in a manner which has stood the test of experiment.

The above equation for the electromotive force of a concentration element, interpreted in the symbols and nomenclature used in the earlier part of this chapter, becomes:

$$\pi = \frac{c - a}{c + a}\ 0.058 \log \frac{p_1}{p_2}\ \text{volts,}$$

where p_1 and p_2 are the osmotic pressures of both cations and anions in the two case. The results show that the electromotive force of a liquid element is always small, being dependent, as will be seen from the formula, mainly upon the relative velocities of the cation and the anion. If these are equal, the electromotive force of such an element would be zero.

Since the electromotive force generated at the surface of contact of electrolytes is very small, we see that the chief source of the electromotive force of primary cells is at the surfaces of contact of the electrodes with the electrolytes.

It was thought for a long time that the chief source of potential was at the surface of contact of the two electrodes, and

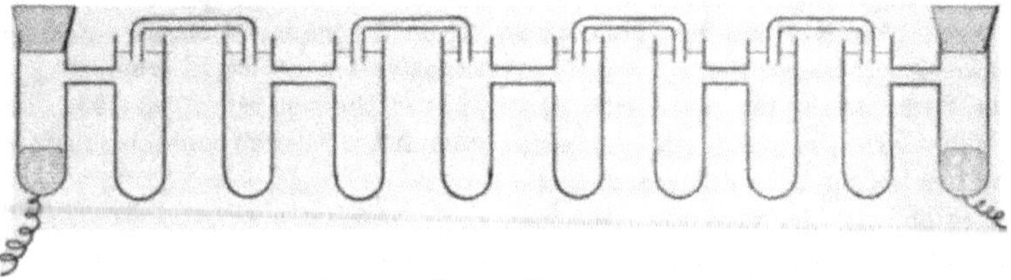

FIG. 12. LIQUID ELEMENT.

solutions of electrolytes which come in contact. The arrangement of the vessels which contain the solutions of electrolytes is given by Nernst, as shown in the accompanying sketch.

The sketch explains itself. The electrodes are inserted into the two ends which contain the same solution, and the three intermediate solutions are inserted between the end solutions, as shown in the sketch.

Nernst calculated the electromotive force of a number of such elements, and compared the results of calculation with those of measurement. He found a satisfactory agreement between the two in every this error persisted until the epoch-making work of Nernst, which we are now studying, appeared in 1889. The voltaic cell was, therefore, discovered about a century before it was understood, and a simple mathematical theory of its action worked out. We have thus far applied the theory to simple primary batteries with one metal as the electrodes. We shall now turn to more complex cells, which are far better known than the simple cases which we have been considering.

A TYPICAL TWO-METAL CELL.

The cells which we have thus far studied are of such simple construction, that they will scarcely be recognized as typical primary batteries, by any one who is not familiar with the later developments in electrochemistry. It should be added that such cells have little or no technical value, since they are incapable of furnishing any considerable amount of electricity for any appreciable time.

The primary cells with which we are ordinarily familiar, consist generally of two different electrodes and two different electrolytes. Where the electrodes are surrounded by their own salts, the theory which we have just considered can be applied to them. Let us take a typical example of a two-metal battery, each metal being surrounded by one of its own salts. In practice, the two metals used differ greatly in their solution-tensions; one having a very great, and the other a very small solution-tension. Let metal A have a very great solution-tension, and be surrounded by one of its own salts; and let metal B have a very small solution-tension, and be surrounded by a solution of one of its salts.

Since the solution-tension of A is very great, it will always be larger than the osmotic pressure of the cations in any solution of any of its salts which can be prepared. This metal will, therefore, throw some ions off into the solution, until the electrical double layer formed establishes equilibrium between the number sent into the solution, and the number which separates from the solution. This metal will, therefore, become negative with respect to the solution, which will be positive. The potential between this metal and the solution will be:

$$\pi_1 = \frac{0.058}{v} \log \frac{P}{p},$$

v being the valence of the metal, P its

solution-tension, and p the osmotic pressure of the metal ions in the solution.

The metal on the other side of the cell has a small solution-tension, and the best results are obtained when the solution-tension of this metal is practically infinitesimal. The osmotic pressure of the metal ions in the solution is, therefore, greater than the solution-tension of this metal, and, consequently, metal will separate from the solution upon the bar. The bar will, therefore, become positive with respect to the solution, which will be negative. The difference in potential between the two will be:

$$\pi_2 = \frac{0.058}{v_1} \log \frac{P_1}{p_1}$$

where v_1 is the valence of the metal, P_1 its solution-tension, and p_1 the osmotic pressure of the metal ions in the solution. The electromotive force of an element constructed of the above two metals, A and B, is the difference between the potentials on the two sides:

$$\pi_1 - \pi_2 = \pi = \frac{0.058}{v} \log \frac{P}{p} - \frac{0.058}{v_1} \log \frac{P_1}{p_1}$$

Since the metals used in constructing primary cells are in general bivalent; $v = v_1 = 2$; when the above expression becomes,

$$\pi = 0.029 \left(\log \frac{P}{p} - \log \frac{P_1}{p_1} \right)$$

This is the formula for calculating the electromotive force of such elements as we are considering. It is only necessary to know the solution-tensions of the two metals in question, and the osmotic pressure of the metal ions in the two solutions, in order to calculate the electromotive force of such a cell. The other factors which come into play, such as the potential at the contact of the two electrolytes, etc., are so small that they can practically be neglected. There are a number of very much more complex elements known, in which we have a metal surrounded by some electrolyte than one of its salts, or carbon surr by a solution of some electrolyte; t cases the theory in hand does not and we are not able to calculate th tromotive force of such combinatic

CHAPTER VII–CALCULATION OF THE ELECTRO-MOTIVE FORCE OF ELEMENTS.

PART III.

DETERMINATION OF THE SOLUTION-TENSION OF METALS.

It is not necessary to know the values of the solution-tensions of the metals used as electrodes, in order to calculate the electromotive force of elements in which the same metal is used on both sides of the cell. This will be seen by examining the equation for the electromotive force of such cells. The solution-tension of the metal used is of the same value on the two sides of the cell, and when the potentials on the two sides are subtracted, the two equal values have opposite signs and, therefore, disappear from the equation.

If, however, we are calculating the electromotive force of an element in which two different metals are used as the electrodes, it is necessary to know the values of the solution-tensions of both metals, since both values appear in the final equation. That such must be the case, can be seen at once from the fact that the solution-tensions of the two metals have different values, and when the two potentials are subtracted these two different values do not disappear. We must now study carefully the method employed in determining the solution-tensions of the different metals.

We have seen that when a metal is immersed in a solution of one of its salts, a difference in potential between the metal and the solution results, the magnitude depending upon the solution-tension of the metal and the osmotic pressure of the metal ions in the solution. A number of methods have been devised for *measuring such differences in potential between metals and electrolytes.* The one in which the drop-electrode was employed can only be referred to.[*] The one which we shall study in some detail involves the use of the "normal electrode."[†]

"This method is based upon the use of an electrode whose potential is known. This is connected with the metal immersed in the solution whose difference in potential it is desired to measure, and the electromotive force of the whole combination determined. Since the potential of the normal electrode is known, that between the metal and the solution in which it is immersed is determined at once; the electromotive force of the two sides when combined, being the difference between the potentials on the two sides. The form of normal electrode used by Ostwald is shown in the accompanying sketch. The bottom of a glass tube, about eight centimetres high and two to two and one-half centimetres in diameter, is covered with mercury. The mercury is covered with a layer of mercurous chloride, and the vessel is then filled with a normal solution of potassium chloride. A platinum wire protruding beyond the end of a glass tube into which it is fused, dips into the mercury and serves as one electrode. The other glass tube passing through the cork, is also filled with normal potassium chlo-

---

[*] Ostwald; *Ztschr. phys. Chem.*, 1, 583

[†] The following account of the use of the normal electrode in measuring differences of potential between metals and electrolytes, is taken from Elements of Physical Chemistry, by H. C. Jones, which will be published in the near future by the Macmillans.

ride. The glass tube at the end of the rubber tube dips into the liquid, whose potential against a given metal immersed in it, is to be measured.

"The metal immersed in the liquid serves as the second electrode.

"The electromotive force of the whole system is now measured. Knowing the

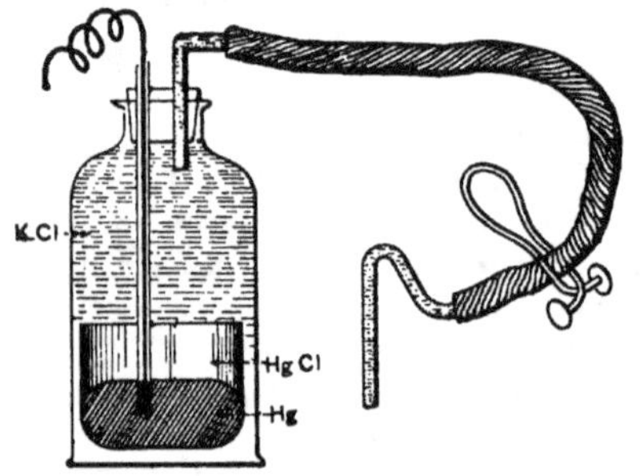

FIG. 18. OSTWALD NORMAL ELECTRODE.

potential on the one side, that on the other is obtained at once. The potential of the normal electrode just described is 0.56 volt. The metal is positive, the electrolyte negative, which means that there is a tendency for the mercury ions present to separate from the solution as metallic mercury, and this is expressed in potential by 0.56 volt. In such measurements the potential of the metal is taken as zero, and that of the electrolyte expressed as either positive or negative. The potential of our normal electrode is, then, — 0.56 volt.

"Differences of potential between metals and electrolytes can be readily measured by means of this normal electrode. Let us take as an example, the difference in potential between magnesium and a normal solution of magnesium chloride. The normal electrode is connected with the normal solution of magnesium chloride,

into which a bar of magnesium dips. The electromotive force of this system was found to be 1.791 volts. The electromotive force of this element, as we know, is expressed thus:

$$\pi = \frac{0.058}{v} \log \frac{P}{p} - 0.058 \log \frac{P_1}{p_1}$$

where P is the solution-tension of magnesium, p the osmotic pressure of the magnesium ions in the solution, 2 the valence of magnesium, P_1 the solution-tension of mercury, and p_1 the osmotic pressure of the mercury ions in the solution.

"We have seen that $0.058 \log \frac{P_1}{p_1} = -$ 0.56 volt, and substituting this value in the above equation we have:

$$\frac{0.058}{v} \log \frac{}{p} = 1.791 - 0.56 \text{ volt} = 1.231 \text{ volts.}$$

Therefore;

$$0.029 \log \frac{P}{p} = 1.231 \text{ volts;}$$

which is the difference in potential between magnesium and a normal solution of magnesium chloride."

Differences of potential between a number of metals and normal or saturated solutions of their salts, have been measured by Neumann.* A few of his results are given below:

	Sulphate.	Chloride.
Magnesium	+ 1.239	+ 1.231
Aluminum	+ 1 040	+ 1 015
Zinc	+ 0.524	+ 0 508
Iron	+ 0.093	+ 0.067
Nickel	— 0.022	— 0.020
Copper	— 0.515	.....
Mercury	— 0.980	.....
Silver	— 0 974	.....
Gold	....	— 1.356
Platinum	.....	— 1 066

The above data show that essentially

*Ztschr. phys Chem., xiv, 229.

the same results are obtained whether the sulphate or chloride is used, and this raises the question as to what effect the *nature of the anion has on the difference in potential between the metal and the solution.* This problem was studied extensively by Neumann, who worked with a large number of salts of thallium, indeed 23 in all, and measured the difference in potential between the metal and its solutions. He concluded that for equally dissociated substances the nature of the anion has no influence on the potential difference.

We now come to the final and most important part of the problem, the *calculation of the solution-tension of metals* from the difference in potential between the metal and the solution of one of its salts. This difference in potential is due, on the one hand, to the solution-tension of the metal, and on the other, to the osmotic pressure of the metal ions in the solution. These forces act in opposition to one another, and the result is the formation of a double layer, which assists the weaker force, and, therefore, the difference in potential with which we have been dealing. If we measure this difference in potential, and know the osmotic pressure of the cations in the solution, we can readily calculate, from considerations already developed, the solution-tension of the metal in question.

The difference in potential between a metal, and a solution of one of its salts in which it is immersed is,

$$\pi = \frac{0.058}{v} \log \frac{P}{p}$$

where v is the valence of the cation, P the solution-tension of the metal, and p the osmotic pressure of the metal ions in

the solution. If we know π, v, and p, we can, of course, calculate P,

$$\log P = \frac{\pi v}{0.058} + \log p.$$

The solution-tensions of a few* of the more common metals, as calculated by the method just described, are given below:

Magnesium	10^{44}	atmospheres.
Zinc	10^{18}	"
Cadmium	10^{7}	"
Iron	10^{9}	
Lead	10^{-2}	"
Copper	10^{-9}	"
Mercury	10^{-16}	"
Silver	10^{-16}	"

We are impressed by the magnitudes of the solution-tensions of the metals. For metals like magnesium, aluminum, zinc, and the like, they are almost inconceivably great; while for metals like copper, mercury, silver, gold, platinum, and the like, the solution-tensions are of infinitesimal value.

The enormous magnitude of the one, and the inconceivably small values of the other metals, would lead one to conclude at first that there must be some error in the method employed in calculating the solution-tensions of the different metals. When, however, these values are introduced into the equations for the electromotive force of elements, the results as calculated agree very satisfactorily with those found by experiments. The above is a strong argument in favor of their general correctness.

ARE THE SOLUTION-TENSIONS OF THE METALS CONSTANT?

The question naturally arose as to whether the solution-tensions of the metals are constants for the different metals, or are they affected by the conditions to which the metals are subjected? Ostwald,

* For a fuller list of solution-tensions, see Le Blanc, Elektrochemie.

who has developed this conception much farther than any one else, concluded in the second chapter of this "Lehrbuch," that the solution-tension of a metal is as constant for the metal as its atomic weight. He regared it as independent even of the nature of the solvent in which the metal was immersed.

Light was thrown on this problem in an unexpected manner by work which was done by Jones in Ostwald's laboratory. An element was constructed containing on the one side a tenth-normal solution of silver nitrate in water, and on the other a tenth-normal solution of silver nitrate in ethyl alcohol. The first object in mind in constructing such an element need not be considered here. It was known that silver nitrate is dissociated by water to a much greater extent than by alcohol, and that, consequently, for solutions of the same concentration the aqueous solution contains many more silver ions than the alcoholic. The osmotic pressure of the silver ions in the aqueous solution would, therefore, be much greater than in the alcoholic solution. The solution-tension of the metal in the two solvents was assumed to be the same.

From these data it would be a perfectly simple matter to determine which side of the element would be positive and which negative; that pole would, of course, be positive, on which silver ions were separating in the form of metal. Since the solution-tension of the metal is the same on both sides of the cell, metal ions will separate from the solution on that side on which the osmotic pressure of the metal ions is the greater. We have just seen that the osmotic pressure of the silver ions in the aqueous solution is the greater; consequently, the pole immersed in

the aqueous solution of silver nitrate would be the positive pole.

The cell was constructed as described, and an attempt was made to measure its electromotive force. The first fact which was discovered, was that the pole immersed in the alcoholic solution of silver nitrate was positive. This was very embarrassing, and, at first, seemed entirely inexplicable. A number of experiments were repeated and all gave the same result. The facts were undoubtedly not in accord with the assumptions which had been made. What was to be done? It was obvious that there was something wrong with the assumptions. We then convinced ourselves beyond all question, that silver nitrate in water is much more strongly dissociated than in alcohol at the same concentration. This left but one assumption untested, and that was, that the solution-tension of the metal is a constant in the different solvents. This assumption must then be wrong, and the experiment was so carried out as to determine the relative solution-tensions of silver in an aqueous, and in an alooholic solution of silver nitrate.

The element was constructed using a tenth-normal solution of silver nitrate in water on the one side, and a tenth-normal solution of silver nitrate in alcohol on the other side. The electromotive force of the combination was measured, and from this the relative solution-tensions calculated, as follows: The potential in the alcoholic solution is expressed thus,

$$\pi_1 = 0.058 \log \frac{p_1}{P_1}$$

The valence of the silver being one, does not enter into the formula, and since silver is an element whose solution-tension is very small, it is less than the osmotic pressure of the silver ions in the solution. Some ions will, therefore, separate from the solution upon the bar, and the solution will be negative with respect to the bar. This changes the sign of the potential, and throws the osmotic pressure in the numerator and the solution-tension in the denominator, which is exactly the reverse of what we had when the solution-tension of the metal was very great with respect to the osmotic pressure of the metal ions in the solution.

The potential between the bar of silver and the aqueous solution of silver nitrate is,

$$\pi_2 = 0.058 \log \frac{p_2}{P_2}$$

The electromotive force of the element as a whole is the difference between the potentials on the two sides:

$$\pi_1 - \pi_2 = \pi = 0.058 \left(\log \frac{p_1}{P_1} - \log \frac{p_2}{P_2} \right)$$

Making P_2, the solution-tension in the aqueous solution, $= 1$, we have,

$$\text{Log } P_1 = -\left(\frac{\pi_1 - \pi_2}{0.058} \right) + \log \frac{p_1}{p_2}$$

Inserting into this equation the values of p_1 and p_2; *i. e.*, the osmotic pressure of the silver ions in the alcohol and aqueous solutions, respectively; we can calculate P_1, the solution-tension of the metal in the alcoholic solution, in terms of the solution-tension in the aqueous solution as unity. The osmotic pressure of the silver ions in the aqueous solution can be readily determined from the conductivity results, being proportional to the dissociation in this solvent. The osmotic pressure of the silver ions in the alcoholic solution can be determined only approximately, since by the conductivity method, as we have seen, we can measure the dissociation of an electrolyte in alco-

hol only approximately. Obtaining this value as accurately as possible, and inserting it in the above equation, we obtain for P_1 the value 0.05. This is in terms of water as unity, and means that the solution-tension of silver in the alcohol solution of its salt, is about one-twentieth of the solution-tension of this metal in the aqueous solution. More recent work by Jones and Smith has shown that the solution-tension of zinc in an aqueous solution of one of its salts, is very different from that in an alcoholic solution of the same salt of the same concentration. The solution-tension of the metals, then, varies from solvent to solvent.

This conception of solution-tension has been extended from the metals to other substances, until we have come to regard solution in general as due to the solution-tension of the soluble substance. In the light of this extension of the term, it is not at all surprising that the solution-tension of a metal varies from solvent to solvent, since we know that the solution-tension or solubility of chemical compounds varies greatly from solvent to solvent. We can, then, regard solution-tension as that force which drives the substance into solution in the solvent; if it is a metal or an electrolyte, the atoms passing over into ions, if a non-electrolyte the molecules dissolve as such in the solvent.

SOME WELL-KNOWN ELEMENTS.

The elements which we have thus far studied give an electromotive force which is unchanged, and are, therefore, known as *constant*. Many of the elements which are used in practice as a means of obtaining electrical energy, have an electromotive force which changes after a time, and are, therefore, known as *inconstant*.

One or two of the more common elements will be considered.

The *Bichromate cell* is a form of battery which finds frequent application in connection with certain kinds of work, and especially in the laboratory. The element consists of a carbon and a zinc electrode, both being immersed in a solution of potassium bichromate and sulphuric acid (chromic acid). The zinc dissolves because of its high solution-tension, and, therefore, this becomes the negative pole or the anode, the carbon being the positive pole. The ions Cr_2O_7 probably yield a few chromium ions of higher valency, which pass over into chromium ions of lower valency, and thus increase the electromotive force of the element. Since the ions Cr_2O_7 are constantly decreasing in number, and the chromium ions of lower valency and also the zinc ions are increasing in number, the electromotive force of this element cannot remain constant.

This agrees with the facts. After the bichromate cell has been used for a time its electromotive force rapidly decreases.

The action of the *Leclanché element*[*] is a little more complex.

"The poles of this useful element are carbon, and manganese dioxide and zinc; the electrolyte, ammonium chloride. The carbon and manganese dioxide are generally mixed with one another. Zinc ions pass into solution, and, consequently, the zinc pole is the anode. The ammonium ions $N\overset{+}{H}_4$ pass over to the cathode, but the hydrogen ions, already present as the result of the dissociation of water, lose their charges more readily than ammonium, and, consequently, separate at the

carbon cathode. The carbon pole would absorb a large amount of hydrogen. The MnO_2 acts as we would expect, as an oxidizing agent. This yields a few $\overset{++++}{Mn}$ ions which tend to pass over into $\overset{++}{Mn}$, by giving up part of their charge to the cathode. We have thus two actions taking place in the Leclanché element, but the electromotive force decreases because the zinc ions become more and more concentrated."

A form of battery which has recently supplanted many of the primary cells in technical work, is known as the *Accumulator or Secondary battery*. These have come into such general use in the last few years, that a word is necessary in reference to the action which takes place in them. Theoretically, we could make an accumulator out of any reversible cell, by simply passing a current through it in the direction opposite to the one in which the current flows when the element is closed. Practical difficulties, however, come into play in a majority of cases, so as to render most such elements useless as accumulators. In practice, the accumulator which is used consists of plates of lead, covered with lead oxide or sulphate, and immersed in a solution of sulphuric acid of a certain specific gravity. When a current is passed through this element, the pole where the current enters becomes covered with lead dioxide, while metallic lead is deposited on the opposite pole. The action of the charging current is, therefore, to convert lead sulphate or oxide into metallic lead at one pole, and into lead dioxide at the other.

If the cell is allowed to discharge, both the metallic lead at the one pole, and the lead dioxide at the other, pass over into lead sulphate in the presence of the sulphuric acid. The chief source of the electromotive force of an accumulator is the passing of quadrivalent lead ions, $\overset{++++}{Pb}$, into bivalent ions, $\overset{++}{Pb}$. The quadrivalent ions, furnished by the lead dioxide, pass over into bivalent, and form with the sulphuric acid, lead sulphate. Metallic lead dissolves at the anode, forming lead ions which carry the positive electricity off from this pole into the solution. With the SO_4 ions of the sulphuric acid these ions form lead sulphate.

The action in the accumulator, on discharging, is exactly the opposite of that which takes place when it is being charged, as we would expect. Charging consists in transforming bivalent lead ions into quadrivalent; while discharging consists in the reverse transformation of quadrivalent lead ions into bivalent.

SOURCES OF THE ELECTRICAL ENERGY IN PRIMARY CELLS.

We should not conclude our study of primary cells, without inquiring into the source of the energy which is converted by them into electrical energy. We know from the law of the conservation of energy that no energy is created or destroyed. Therefore, the large amount of energy which appears as electrical energy in such cells, must come from some other source of energy; the transformation being effected in the cell itself.

Take the element which we first studied in detail—the concentration element. What is the source of the electrical energy in such a cell? We have a certain amount of zinc in each electrode, and a certain amount of zinc chloride on each side of the cell. As the cell gives out electrical energy, or, as we usually say, as the cell acts, zinc dissolves on one side, and just as much zinc separates from the solution on to the bar, on the other side. The one solution of zinc chloride becomes more concentrated, and the other, by just the same amount, more dilute. After the cell has been closed for any length of time that we choose, the amount of zinc chloride in solution on the two sides of the cell is exactly the same as when the cell was first closed, and the amount of zinc in the two electrodes is exactly the same as at the outset. The condition of the zinc chloride and of the zinc is exactly the same, from a chemical standpoint, after the cell has been in operation as before it was closed. The chemical energy in the metal and in the solutions is, therefore, the same after the cell has been in operation as before. The electrical energy which has appeared in the cell, then, cannot come from chemical energy which has disappeared as the result of action which has taken place between the constituents. Since the electrical energy which has appeared cannot come from chemical energy which has disappeared (none having disappeared), it must come from some external source. Such elements have the power of taking up energy in the form of heat from external objects, and converting it into electrical energy; and this is probably the chief source of the electrical energy which appears in such cells.

In other forms of primary cells, however, chemical energy does disappear. This applies to all the more common forms of such cells, and especially to those which are capable of yielding any appreciable quantity of electrical energy. It will be remembered that the concentration elements can only furnish a very small amount of electrical energy. All primary elements which have any considerable technical value, must be capable of furnishing a considerable quantity of electricity at a fairly high potential, say about a volt. The electrical energy, as we have seen, is equal to the quantity multiplied by the potential. When the electrical energy is large some chemical or intrinsic energy must disappear.

If we study the action which takes place in any element like the Grove, Bunsen, Daniell, Leclanché, etc., we shall find that the substances which are present in the cell are in a very different condition, chemically, after the cell has been acting for a considerable time, than before such action took place. The amount of metal in one or both electrodes has changed; or metal has been deposited on one electrode and dissolved from the other; and since the electrodes are of different metals, this would represent a different amount of chemical energy in the system as a whole. And, further, the condition of things in solution has very greatly changed. There is frequently more of one metal in solution after the cell has been acting than before, and less of the other metal; and this would represent a very ditrerent condition with respect to the amount of chemical energy present in the system.

Such elements as these transform chemical energy into electrical; but there is still one question unanswered. Does the transformation take place quantitatively? That is, does all the chemical energy which disappears in such elements appear as electrical energy? And this suggests as a corollary the further question, does all the electrical energy which appears come from the chemical energy? A moment's thought will show that these two questions are not the same.

The first question has been answered by Lord Kelvin and Helmholtz, both theoretically by thermodynamics and practically by experiment. All of the chemical energy which disappears in the cell is not necessarily converted into electrical energy. Some of it may be converted into heat and escape in this form. We know of many elements which give out heat energy as well as electrical energy, and, indeed, most of the primary elements of any technical value belong to this class.

The same investigators have answered the second question. They have shown that all the electrical energy which appears in a primary cell, does not necessarily come from the chemical or intrinsic energy which disappears. A primary cell may have the power of converting, also, some heat energy into electrical energy, and the amount of electrical energy furnished by the cell may be greater than the amount of chemical energy which has disappeared in the cell. Such elements take up the heat energy from surrounding objects, and, consequently, become colder as the action of the cell proceeds. These temperature coefficients of primary cells are, however, not usually very great; the amount of heat energy generated in the one, or the amount used up in the other, being comparatively small.

We may say, then, in general, that the chief source of the electrical energy which appears in the well-known forms of primary cells, is the chemical energy of the substances present in the cell as electrodes and electrolytes. Such cells may, however, convert some of the chemical energy into heat energy which escapes, or may take up heat energy from surrounding objects and convert it into electrical energy.

CONCLUSION.

In the preceding chapters we saw how the laws of gas-pressure apply to the osmotic pressure of solutions; we traced the rise of the theory of electrolytic dissociation and made a few applications of it to chemical problems. In the subsequent chapters I have endeavored to show how these two epoch-making generalizations have been applied, especially to electrochemical problems. Light has been thrown, by means of the theory of electrolytic dissociation, on the whole subject of electrolysis and the electrolytic decomposition of substances in solution. Before this theory was proposed our knowledge was limited mainly to the facts, and such generalizations as had been reached, while they may in some cases have contained an element of truth, were entirely insufficient and unsatisfactory.

The relation between our theory and the velocities with which the ions move, is too obvious to call for any comment.

Since the conducting power of an electrolyte is due entirely to the ions which are present, new light has been thrown on this entire field by the theory of ions. Indeed, some of the most interesting applications of the conductivity of electrolytes have had to do, directly or indirectly, with the determination of the amount of dissociation of the substance which conducted the current. The relation between dissociation and dilution of the solution has always been, and is still, of more than the average interest; and the dissociating power of different solvents is a problem of great importance, about which our knowledge is, in many cases, still scarcely more than qualitative. It is obvious that all such questions have been opened up by the theory of electrolytic dissociation.

When we come to the calculation of the electromotive force of elements, we see what the two great generalizations which form the foundation of these papers, have done. This most important chapter of electrochemistry has been created since these generalizations were reached, and as the direct result of their application. We can now interpret, in terms of them, the action of the primary cell, and have an insight, for the first time, into what takes place in the battery, which was discovered by Volta more than a century ago.

These are but relatively few of the applications of these generalizations to electrochemical problems. If we were to inquire into their applications in other directions, we should find that they are just as numerous and important. The whole science of the new physical chemistry, which has grown up in the last fifteen years, centres around these generalizations; and more has been done in this period to place chemistry upon an exact mathematical basis, and to correlate it with the only exact science, physics, than was accomplished before this time in the whole history of the science. To follow any farther this line of thought would lead us beyond the scope of these chapters, and must be left to the student of the whole field of physical chemistry, of which electrochemistry is only a part, but an important part.

INDEX.